MARILYN KAYE

REAL HEROES

GULLIVER BOOKS

HARCOURT BRACE JOVANOVICH

San Diego   New York   London

Requests for permission to make copies of any part of the work
should be mailed to: Permissions Department,
Harcourt Brace Jovanovich, Publishers, 8th Floor,
Orlando, Florida 32887.

Library of Congress Cataloging-in-Publication Data
Kaye, Marilyn.
Real heroes/Marilyn Kaye.—1st ed.
p. cm.
"Gulliver books."
Summary: When his father joins other parents in demonstrating
against a teacher who is HIV-positive, Kevin is torn between his
loyalty to his father whom he has always considered a hero and his
admiration for his favorite sixth grade teacher.
ISBN 0-15-200563-3
[1. Fathers and sons—Fiction. 2. Homosexuality—Fiction.
3. Teacher–student relationships—Fiction.] I. Title.
PZ7.K2127Rc 1993
[Fic]—dc20   92-39610

Designed by Lisa Peters
Printed in the United States of America
First edition
A B C D E

For my father, Harold S. Kaye

CHAPTER ONE

"It's your move, Kevin," Emily says.

"I know, I know." Kevin looks at the board. The pattern of red and black disks makes no particular sense to him. But Emily's waiting, so he makes his move.

Emily promptly jumps him. "King me."

Kevin obliges. Then he pushes another disk forward. While Emily examines the board, he looks through the picture window at the house next door, his house. The driveway is empty, just as it has been all day.

"Kevin!" There's a hint of impatience in Emily's voice. "You're not paying attention."

With a silent sigh, he turns back to the board. Checkers has never been one of his favorite games. It's slow. You're supposed to look ahead, weigh the possibilities, compare the positions. You have to ask yourself questions: If I do this, what can she do? There's too much thinking and guessing. Kevin prefers Nintendo, or anything that involves making quick moves, fast decisions. He likes the kind of games in which you can't afford the time to weigh the consequences.

But Emily likes checkers, this is Emily's living room, and anything's better than going back to that empty house next door. Kevin pretends to study the board.

"I saw your friend Eric this morning," Emily remarks.

"Yeah? Where?"

"Outside Woolworth's. He showed me a comic book and he claimed he swiped it." She sniffs. "I'll bet he didn't. He was just trying to shock me."

Kevin grins. "Yeah, probably. Sounds like Eric."

"Doesn't that bother you?" Emily asks. "He thinks it's cool to steal something."

"It's just his way of being funny," Kevin says. He knows Emily doesn't like Eric and the feeling's mutual. Emily thinks Eric is a pushy show-off with a nasty mouth, and there are times when Kevin agrees. But he has to come to Eric's defense, since they've been hanging out together since they were little kids.

Eric thinks Emily is a know-it-all and the most conceited girl in their sixth-grade classroom. Having lived next door to her most of his life, Kevin knows better. She's smart, for sure, but she doesn't giggle or act goofy like most other girls.

He shoves one of his few remaining checkers onto a square.

"You sure you want to do that?" Emily asks.

She was giving him the chance to take it back, and he can see why. It was a dumb move. But he'd just as soon get the game over with. "Yeah."

Lifting her checker, Emily counts aloud as she leaps over his remaining men. "One, two, three. I win."

Kevin fakes a little dismay for her. "Damn."

"Don't cuss," Emily says primly, but he can tell she's satisfied by the response. He doesn't mind losing to her because he knows she won't go bragging about it to kids at school.

For a girl, Emily can be pretty cool. She doesn't gossip. As far as he knows, she never told anyone about the time Kevin went outside to get the newspaper and locked himself out of the house in his pajamas. Or about how she saw Kevin's father throw a screaming fit the day Kevin's mother walked out.

Everyone knows his mother's gone. Emily knows even more than the others. Their mothers had been best friends. But he can trust her not to talk about it with any of her dopey girl friends. Or with him.

He gets up and goes to the window. It's getting dark out, and the driveway across the lawn is still deserted. "Em, what time is it?"

"Quarter after five," she tells him. "What time does your father get home today?"

"His shift was over at three. He might be doing a double shift, but he usually comes home first."

She joins him at the window. "Don't worry, I'm sure he's okay."

"Of course he's okay," he snaps.

"Well, he *is* a police officer," she says. "That's not exactly the safest job in the world. Even in a town like Greendale."

"He's always been a police officer," Kevin reminds her. "Why would I start worrying about that now?"

"Well, I was thinking, now that it's just the two of you," she begins, but she catches herself in time and shuts up. "You want to play another game?"

"Nah, let's watch TV."

"Kevin, you know I'm only allowed one hour of television a day, and I'm saving it for tonight."

"But it's Saturday," Kevin protests.

"That doesn't make any difference to my parents. And I have to finish my homework before I can watch tonight."

"Homework," Kevin groans. Their teacher piles it on. He tries to cheer himself by saying, "Just one more week of school and we'll be on Christmas break. No homework for ten days."

Emily looks out the window. "I wish we could have some snow. Wouldn't it be nice to have a white Christmas for a change?"

Kevin rolls his eyes. "This is Georgia, Em, remember? We've never had snow at Christmas."

"I can wish, can't I?" she counters.

"If wishes were horses, then beggars would ride," he replies automatically. Then he remembers who always said that and he wishes he could take it back.

A car pulls into Emily's driveway, and a moment later, Emily's mother walks in. "Hi, kids." She tosses her coat and some shopping bags onto a chair.

"Hi, Mom," Emily says.

"Hello, Mrs. Payne," Kevin says, still watching his own driveway.

Mrs. Payne goes over to the Christmas tree and turns on its lights. "Hungry?"

Kevin and Emily follow her into the kitchen. She pours out some milk and opens a cookie jar.

"These are great," Emily says, sticking her hand in the jar. "Mom made them last night."

"It's your mother's recipe," Mrs. Payne tells Kevin.

Kevin's hand hovers over the jar. He knows those cookies, with the chocolate and butterscotch chips.

"Take one," Mrs. Payne urges.

Well, it's just her recipe. It isn't as if *she* made

them. He chews fast, trying not to enjoy it too much. He's uncomfortably aware of their eyes on him. What do they think he's going to do, burst into tears from the taste of a cookie? He's way beyond that now.

But Mrs. Payne is giving him that awful look, and he knows what's coming. "Kevin, dear, I know how you must miss your mother. And I know how hard it is for you to understand, but she had a reason for doing what she did. She wants to talk to you about it, and she's very upset that you won't see her or talk to her."

He pops the rest of the cookie in his mouth. "I have to go now."

Mrs. Payne shakes her head, but she gives up. "Won't you stay for dinner, Kevin?"

"No, thank you," he replies. "See ya, Em."

He used to like Mrs. Payne. But he doesn't want to talk, and he doesn't want to listen, because there's no point. It's not going to change anything. He doesn't want to think about it, he doesn't even want to hear that word—*mother*. In fact, he prefers the word his father uses for her—*bitch*. Of course, if he ever used that word in front of his father, he'd be in serious trouble. Or maybe not.

Crossing the lawn, he sees the old Chevy pickup coming up the road. In the dusky twilight, he makes out three figures in the car. He brightens. Maybe his father went out with a couple of his buddies for a beer or two. That's a good sign.

His father gets out of the car, and Kevin's spirits soar. Charley Delaney is smiling. It's not one of those clenched-teeth smiles he's managed to produce over the past couple of months. It's a real smile.

"Hi, Dad."

"Hey, buddy-boy," he says and tousles Kevin's hair. "Been over to the Paynes'?"

"Yes, sir." Kevin watches anxiously for signs of disapproval. His father isn't too crazy about Mrs. Payne anymore either. "Hello, Mr. Fields. Hi, Will."

Will salutes him with an easy grin. He puts a hand on his hip, pulling his jacket back and revealing his gun. According to Charley Delaney, Will does this because he's a rookie and he's showing off a little. But he's a good guy, Will Garner, and Kevin likes him.

Kevin is not as partial to Mr. Fields, Eric's dad. Mr. Fields chews tobacco and he makes cracks about how short Kevin is for his age. But the other cops think he's funny, and he makes Charley Delaney laugh, so Kevin doesn't mind having him around.

"Got a surprise for you, Kev," Charley says. "Give me a hand, Will."

Kevin follows them to the back of the truck, and what he sees there makes him feel better than he's felt in ages. It's a Christmas tree, a big, fat one.

"Dad, that's great. That's really great."

"Bet you thought I forgot all about Christmas, huh? Not on your life, buddy-boy."

Charley and Will hoist the tree on their shoulders and start toward the house. Mr. Fields retrieves a paper bag from the car and follows them. Kevin brings up the rear. Once inside, he runs around turning on lights. The whole living room is coated with dust, but it doesn't look so bad in the artificial light.

"Watch it!" Will yells as they lean the tree against a wall, tipping a lamp in the process. Charley reaches to grab the lamp, leaving Will to steady the tree. They both start laughing.

Kevin had almost forgotten the sound of his father's hearty laugh. Mr. Fields pulls a six-pack out of the bag and cracks open a beer.

"How about some music?" Will asks.

Kevin looks at his father. Music, like Charley's laugh, is something that hasn't been heard in this house for a while. Charley hesitates, then nods, and Kevin makes a mad dash to the tape deck. He can sense his father's eyes on him and he knows he must choose carefully. No mushy stuff, of course. But the harder part is finding a cassette that doesn't have any particular memories attached to it. He settles on some jazzed-up Christmas carols. *She* never liked that one.

"Kevin, where are the lights and ornaments? And the tree stand?"

"In the attic, Dad. I'll get them."

"I'll give you a hand," Will says. He follows Kevin to the second floor and then up the narrow stairs to the attic.

"I think they're over here," Kevin says, pushing aside an old trunk.

"You should have seen your old man today," Will tells him as they examine boxes. "My partner and I get a call about a holdup at the Seven-Eleven, right? It turns out to be a couple of loonies, but one of them's got a knife, and he's waving it around. I call for backup, and your dad shows up. He walks up to this jerk and takes the knife right out of his hand." He whistles. "What a guy."

His words are sweeter than the tune wafting up from downstairs. There's a lump in Kevin's throat and he's afraid to speak, so he just nods.

"It seems to me," Will goes on, "that he's back to his old self."

Please, Kevin prays. Please.

But back downstairs, Kevin is still a little nervous when they start opening the boxes. *She* was a real Christmas freak, and he's afraid of what certain ornaments might spark in his father's head. When Charley pulls out the lopsided angel she made in a ceramics class, Kevin starts to sweat.

He's going to throw it against the wall. Like the vase.

But he doesn't. He barely glances at the doll as he hands it to Will, who's setting up the ladder. "This goes on top."

Kevin lets out the breath he's been holding for two months. It's over. The black moods, the grim silences, the creak of footsteps late at night when Charley roams the house like a lonely ghost.

Mr. Fields is leaning against the mantel, where Kevin has lined up the Christmas cards. And something else, too.

"This your report card?" he asks.

"Yes, sir," Kevin replies.

"All A's," his father announces.

Mr. Fields examines the card closely. "I see an A minus. In *P.E.!* What's the matter, Kevin? Having a little trouble shooting hoops?" His tone is innocent, but his lips are curled in a sneer. Kevin stiffens.

Charley comes to his defense. "Kevin's gonna grow. I didn't shoot up till I was fourteen." He was bending down, adjusting the tree stand, but he stands as he says this, giving Mr. Fields a good look at his full six and a half feet.

It's a comfort to Kevin to know he's going to grow, but he still has three years of being a runt to look forward to. At least Charley's remark shuts up Mr. Fields. He knows better than to irritate Charley Delaney.

"We had gymnastics this term," Kevin says. He

can't resist adding, "Didn't Eric tell you?" He knows full well that Eric doesn't have the same kind of relationship with his father that Kevin has with Charley.

"Gymnastics," Mr. Fields snorts. "What's that, somersaults?"

"Parallel bars," Kevin says. "And a vault."

"That why you got a minus?" Mr. Fields asks. "Couldn't get enough height to make it over the vault?"

"Sort of," Kevin mumbles.

Mr. Fields snickers. "I'll bet old Coach Harris gave you plenty of grief for that."

Doesn't Eric tell him anything? Kevin wonders. "Coach Harris retired last year. We have Mr. Logan now. He's great; all the kids like him."

The men start talking cop talk, so Kevin concentrates on untangling the strings of lights and thinks about that P.E. class. This past term was the first time he could remember really liking P.E. Old Coach Harris had been awful, always screaming at them and blowing his stupid whistle and making cracks about Kevin's puny build.

Mr. Logan is different. He's a lot younger for one thing. He's down to earth, a regular guy, and he acts as if he really likes being with kids. He was nice about Kevin's problems with the vault. He seemed to understand how embarrassed Kevin was, and he never criticized him in front of the others. He gave Kevin extra help after school.

11

Two months ago, when Kevin's world blew up, he thought about talking to Mr. Logan. Mr. Logan knew something was wrong because Kevin couldn't keep his mind on anything. But he didn't bug Kevin about it. He just told Kevin that if he wanted to talk about whatever it was, he'd be glad to listen. Kevin almost did. He didn't, because he got his concentration back. But if he ever needed to talk to anyone about how he felt, he'd probably talk to Mr. Logan.

They get to work on the tree. Even before it's decorated, the tree brightens the room, making it look more like a home where a family lives and eats and sleeps and has Christmas.

"Kev?"

"Yeah, Dad?"

"What do you want to do about dinner?"

Kevin looks at his father blankly. "Dinner?"

"Yeah," his father says. "Dinner."

Dinner. For two months, dinner for Kevin has consisted of bologna sandwiches or a heated-up casserole from Mrs. Payne next door. He has no idea what his father's been eating. He's been doing double shifts.

"Aren't you going back to the station?" he asks.

"No. One shift a day from now on. How about we order a pizza? You guys want pizza?"

"Not me," Mr. Fields says. "I gotta get home." Kevin's not sorry to see him leave. Mr. Fields can be funny sometimes, but he can also be nasty. Eric's like that too. At least Kevin can stand up to Eric. There's not much a kid can do about a nasty grown-up.

Charley calls to order the pizza while Will and Kevin continue tossing tinsel on the tree. It's a big tree, and they're not finished when the pizza arrives. They move into the kitchen and set it on the table.

"Tell me, Will," Charley says. "What do single guys do about meals? You can't live on pizza and Kentucky Fried Chicken."

"You learn to cook," Will says. "I make a pretty mean meat loaf, if I say so myself."

"You hear that, Kev? Tomorrow we go to the supermarket, and we start cooking."

"Okay, Dad."

His father keeps talking, but it's like he's talking more to himself than to Kevin. "It's just you and me now, buddy-boy. We're all we've got. So we're going to take care of each other from now on."

"Right," Kevin says. Nothing would make him happier than spending more time with his father. There's no one like Charley Delaney. There's no one tougher or braver or smarter. Good-looking, too. Everyone likes Charley Delaney. Everyone respects him. Right this minute, he's telling Will about something, and Will looks like he practically worships Kevin's father. All the rookies were like that. Kevin remembers visits to the police station, watching how all the cops looked at Charley with admiration, listening to the way they always asked his opinion. Kevin can look at his father and see himself, all grown-up.

There was only one person in the world who didn't admire and respect Charley Delaney. One person who could make him act weird and depressed and not like himself. But she's gone. And Charley's back.

They're just finishing the pizza when the phone rings. Charley picks it up. "Delaney," he barks. Sometimes Kevin practices saying his last name like that, but his voice isn't up for it yet.

"They're starting a father-son bowling league at the station," Will tells Kevin. "You and your daddy gonna sign up?"

"I don't know. Dad hasn't said anything about it. I hope so."

Kevin realizes his father's been silent. He looks up. His father is extending the phone in Kevin's direction. He doesn't say "It's Eric," or "It's Andy," or any of Kevin's buddies. But Kevin knows who it is by the awful line that's creasing Charley's forehead, by the way his lips are pressed together.

"You want to talk to her?" he asks Kevin.

Kevin tries to read his father's eyes, but they're icy-blue cold now and Kevin can't see anything at all. He swallows, hard. Then he shakes his head, no.

Charley nods. It's the right answer. "He doesn't want to talk to you, Marie." He hangs up the phone

14

and returns to the table. Will is picking at a piece of pizza crust. Kevin feels his father's hand on his shoulder, and he turns.

There's no more ice in his eyes. They're clear and warm. "C'mon, buddy-boy. Let's get back to that tree."

CHAPTER TWO

Every now and then, very early in the morning, Kevin thinks he hears her. In those dim moments when he's no longer sleeping but not yet awake, his fuzzy brain conjures up sounds. Sometimes it's an off-key tune filtering out from the bathroom. At other times, it's the clatter of pans from the kitchen. Once in a while, he thinks he hears her crying.

Then he's completely awake, and there are no more sounds. For one split second, a wave of heaviness creeps over him. But that doesn't last long. All he has to do is drum up an image of his father, and the sadness is replaced by something hot and cold and fierce.

On this particular day, he can't waste time feeling

anything at all. His father has been on the day shift all week, and Kevin has gotten into the habit of seeing him off. He pulls on a bathrobe, but he doesn't bother to search for his slippers. He doesn't have to wear them now because the floors aren't dirty anymore. Last week, Charley hired a lady, Ms. Tolliver, to come in most afternoons to clean and sometimes fix dinner.

Downstairs in the kitchen, Charley is bent over his coffee with his usual morning expression, but he manages something sort of like a smile for Kevin. "Morning, son." He nods toward the box of cereal and carton of milk on the table.

"Good morning, Dad." Kevin helps himself to cereal and milk and sits down. He knows that Charley Delaney doesn't much care for conversations in the morning, but that's okay. He enjoys just looking at his father in the morning. Freshly shaved, smelling of soap, his uniform clean and pressed, his gleaming badge. Right now, the eyes are listless, but soon, as Charley drinks his coffee, they'll become bright and alert.

Only in the past week has Kevin observed so much about his father. Being aware of all these details makes him feel closer to Charley, more attached. He'd always loved his father, but this is something more.

The eyes were starting to come alive now. "Shouldn't you be getting ready for school?" Charley asks Kevin.

"It's Christmas break," Kevin reminds him. "I'm going to Atlanta today, remember?"

Charley snaps his fingers. "Oh, right, you're shopping for Christmas gifts with Eric and the Rollins kid, right? What's his name?"

"Andy. Mrs. Rollins is dropping us off at the mall and picking us up later."

"You'll need some money," his father says. He reaches into his pocket and gets his battered wallet.

"I think I've got enough; I've been saving from my allowance," Kevin says, but his father pushes bills across the table.

"I want you to pick up something for your aunt and uncle and their kids, okay? We'll be going there for Christmas Eve dinner."

Kevin nods. They only see Charley's sister and her family a couple of times a year since they live two hours away and Charley doesn't get along all that well with his sister, anyway. But they always spend Christmas Eve together, and they always exchange gifts.

"What should I get them?"

"I don't know, anything." Maybe he feels guilty about making Kevin do this because he shoves a few more bills at him.

"Thanks, Dad."

Charley winks. "It's a bribe. Don't get me another one of those Hawaiian ties, okay?"

Kevin grins. "Dad, I was five years old!"

Charley puts on his hat. "Well, I'd better get moving before the bad guys get a head start on me."

He looks so official now, so important and serious. The bad guys don't stand a chance. He pauses in the doorway. "Oh, I signed us up for the bowling league. We play on Saturdays. Okay with you?"

"Great," Kevin says. With his father gone, he hastily finishes his breakfast and washes his bowl. Putting the milk back in the refrigerator, he sees the remnants of the lasagna he and Charley made a couple of days ago. He remembers how they laughed as they struggled with those noodles that stuck together. Good times like that—they wouldn't have been possible before. So maybe every cloud really does have a silver lining.

He showers and dresses, and now there's nothing to do but wait for Mrs. Rollins to pick him up. He turns on the TV. It's all boring stuff, cartoons and news and those dumb shows where people sit around talking about problems. He leaves it on for the noise, but he gets a pad and pencil and starts to list the people he has to buy presents for.

Dad. Andy and Eric. Uncle Mitch and Aunt Louise. His younger cousins, Steven and Jennifer. Emily. He and Emily have exchanged gifts since they were little, but he'll have to get away from his buddies to get hers. A Christmas card for his classroom teacher, Miss Anthony, and maybe one for Mr. Logan, too.

He collects his allowance savings, adds the money

Charley gave him, and counts it. He's got more than last year, and there's one less person to buy for. So he'll be okay.

Something on the TV catches his ear, and he looks up. "Evil stepmothers," the white-haired man is saying. "Myth or reality? Can any woman overcome the stereotype perpetuated by fairy tales? Today, we're talking to three real-life stepmothers whose experiences might shed some light on this."

Kevin wonders if he'll have to deal with a stepmother one of these days. He noticed the way women looked at Charley when they went to the supermarket together last week. He doesn't think this is something he has to worry about for a long time. He doubts that marriage has much appeal for his father right now.

A car honks outside. He turns off the TV, grabs his jacket, and runs out. He gets in the back of the car, next to Eric.

"Good morning, Kevin," Mrs. Rollins says. She turns around from the driver's seat. "How are you? How's your father?"

She's got that look on her face, that oh-you-poor-little-motherless-boy look. He's seen that look on the face of every mother of every kid he knows. It doesn't bother him today, though. He's in too good a mood.

"We're fine, thank you," he replies. "Hi, guys."

Andy and Eric mumble greetings. It's almost an hour's ride to Atlanta, and there's not much they can say to each other with Andy's mother in the car. So they kill time discussing the game that was on TV the night before and arguing over who had the best jump shot.

When they reach the mall, they endure Mrs. Rollins's instructions and warnings. "Remember, boys, this is the big city, so you're not going to talk to any strangers."

"I guess we can't ask any salespeople for help, then," Andy says. "They're strangers."

"Don't sass me, young man," his mother reprimands. "Now, I want you all to keep together and stay out of trouble, you hear me?"

"We hear you," Andy says.

"You don't have to worry about us, Mrs. Rollins," Eric states. "Kevin and me, we brought our dads' guns."

"He's just making a joke, Mrs. Rollins," Kevin interjects quickly.

Mrs. Rollins sighs. "I'll pick y'all up right here at four o'clock. Is someone wearing a watch?"

They finally escape and head into the mall. It's packed with shoppers. Every store displays fancy decorations and sparkling lights, and Christmas carols fill the air. "Where do you guys want to go first?" Andy asks.

"Lunch," Eric says. "I'm hungry."

"It's not even eleven o'clock," Andy protests.

"So what, I'm hungry."

"You hungry?" Andy asks Kevin.

"Not particularly," Kevin replies. But they end up at Burger King anyway, because Eric wants to eat and Eric gets his way. The other two know from experience that if they don't go along with him, he'll make them both miserable. There are some times when Kevin wonders why he and Andy hang out with Eric. Habit, probably, because they've been hanging out since second grade.

"How much money you got?" Eric asks the others as they eat.

"Sixty dollars," Kevin tells him.

Andy whistles. "I only have forty, and I have to get presents for my parents and my sister. And Jason."

At the mention of his brother, Andy averts his eyes, and Kevin concentrates on rearranging the tomato slice on his hamburger. Like Kevin's mother, Andy's brother is not a good subject for conversation. But Eric's upper lip curls, and he smirks. *He's going to say something,* Kevin thinks. So he glares at Eric, and Eric backs down.

"I don't know what to get my father," Eric says. "You guys got any ideas?"

"I was thinking about getting mine a wallet," Kevin says. "I don't know."

"What about a book?" Andy suggests. "I might get my father a book about gardening."

"Gardening?" The way Eric's voice rises with that word, Kevin suspects a crack is coming. But Andy faces him squarely.

"Yeah, he likes to garden." His expression dares Eric to make fun of this.

Kevin speaks quickly. "Hey, you know, maybe I should get my father a cookbook. He tried to fix lasagna a couple of days ago." He makes a gagging noise.

"Fathers are hard to buy presents for," Andy muses. "Mothers are a lot easier. You can always get perfume. . . ." His voice trails off, and he looks away again. "Sorry," he mumbles to the wall but really to Kevin.

"Come on, let's get going," Eric says.

They stop first at a record store, where Andy buys a cassette for his sister. Kevin notices a cassette he thinks Emily wants, and he makes a mental note to come back later when he can get away from the guys. He picks up *Greatest Disco Hits of the Seventies* for his uncle.

From there, they move on to the bookstore.

"Hey, guys, check this out." Eric points to a large book on display. The title screams: *Sex and How to Have it Right.* "I'll bet it's got pictures," he says and reaches for it.

"Eric, don't," Kevin hisses. A saleslady is watching them. Besides, there's some sort of band wrapped around the book that would make it impossible to open anyway.

"You're a wimp," Eric accuses him, but he drops his arm. "Hey, did you guys hear about what we're doing in P.E. when we go back?" He wiggles his eyebrows up and down. "Sex education."

"It's *health* education," Andy corrects him.

Eric snickers. "Yeah, but I'll bet it's not going to be about the four major food groups."

"You're probably right," Andy says.

"How do you know about it?" Kevin asks Andy.

"I heard my parents talking. There was some big fuss about it at the last PTA meeting. I want to find the gardening books."

Kevin selects a Sesame Street book for one of his cousins, and Eric gets a paperback romance for his sister. They all pay for their stuff and leave.

"What's going on down there?" Eric asks, leaning over a railing.

Kevin sees a group of people carrying signs and chanting something, but he can't make out what they're saying. They're all wearing red ribbons on their shirts. "It looks like a demonstration."

"Let's check it out," Andy suggests. They get on the escalator. As they move down, the words of the demonstrators become clearer.

"Be safe, be sure—help find a cure! Be safe, be sure—help find a cure!"

They step off the escalator. There's a pretty good sized crowd there. Shoppers pass. Some glance curiously, some linger, some look the other way. A few give money to a man sitting at a table.

"Oh, it's about AIDS," Eric says. He sounds disappointed. Probably because it's an orderly demonstration, Kevin thinks, and there doesn't appear to be any possibility of a riot breaking out.

They start moving around the crowd. Eric edges closer to Kevin. "You think they're all queers?" he whispers.

Kevin shrugs. "How would I know? Let's go to the Gap."

Eric stops suddenly.

"What's the matter?" Andy asks.

Eric opens his mouth, then snaps it shut. "Nothing."

But Kevin's seen what Eric has seen, too. It's Jason Rollins, Andy's brother. He's holding a sign and talking to the guy at the table. Kevin glances at Andy. He can tell Andy's seen him, too. He wonders if Andy wants to speak to his brother. He won't do it if his buddies are around.

"I have an idea," Kevin says. "Why don't we split up for say, an hour, so we can get our presents for each other?"

"Yeah, okay," Andy says quickly. Eric agrees, too. They arrange to meet in front of the Gap at two.

Once he feels he's far enough away, Kevin looks back at the demonstration. He can see Andy talking with Jason. He doesn't blame Andy for not wanting him and Eric around. Andy's embarrassed about Jason, even though it's no secret; they all know Jason's gay.

Of course, Kevin and Eric feel sorry for Andy. Back when they were little kids, Andy used to talk about his big brother all the time, how he was captain of the soccer team and editor of his college newspaper and all that. But now, having a twenty-three-year-old brother who works for a gay magazine isn't exactly something to brag about.

Kevin peers into a few store windows. He's supposed to be using this time to buy presents for Andy and Eric, but he also wants to look for his father's gift. He wants to choose carefully and well, and he doesn't want the guys to see him fussing about that. He's still thinking about a wallet, but a wallet seems so ordinary.

He's standing at a counter in a men's clothing store, looking at the wallets in the glass display and feeling sick about the prices, when he hears his name. "Kevin?"

He turns. "Mr. Logan! What are you doing here?"

He flushes. "I'm sorry. I guess I'm just surprised to see you."

His P.E. teacher grins. "It's strange to see a teacher outside of school, isn't it? Once, when I was about your age, I saw my teacher in a drugstore buying aspirin. And I was stunned to think that she was just a regular person who got headaches."

Kevin nods fervently. He marvels at how this guy reads minds. "Yeah, I mean, yes sir."

Mr. Logan holds up the tie in his hand. "What do you think of this?"

Kevin can't think of anything to say about it. It's just an ordinary tie, dark blue with a thin red stripe. "It's nice," he says politely.

"You mean boring, right? I think so, too. So it's perfect for a boring cousin. What are you looking for?"

"A present for my father," Kevin tells him. "I was thinking about a wallet."

"That's always a useful gift." Mr. Logan leans over and peers into the glass case. "Wow. Expensive."

"I know," Kevin says glumly. "I didn't think they cost that much. But I don't know what else to get him."

"Does your father have any hobbies? What does he do for a living?"

"He's a police officer. And he doesn't have any hobbies. I mean, he doesn't collect stamps or anything. He likes football and basketball."

"A book about sports?" Mr. Logan suggests.

"I don't know," Kevin murmurs. "That's not . . . special."

"I'll tell you what," Mr. Logan says. "I haven't had lunch yet, and I don't think well on an empty stomach. Want to join me?"

Kevin walks with him to an open air café across the mall, where they sit down. While Mr. Logan studies the menu, Kevin takes furtive glances at him. In jeans and a sweater, he looks younger than he does at school. His manner is the same, friendly and relaxed.

Kevin knows he can get mad, but not the way other teachers get mad. He doesn't yell. He recalls one time in the gym when fat Joey Aldrich tried to tumble and did a belly flop on the mat. Some of the guys snickered. Mr. Logan didn't raise his voice when he told them to stop, but he gave it an edge that made it crack like a whip. No one ever laughed at anyone else again.

Mr. Logan orders a grilled cheese sandwich and iced tea, and Kevin asks for a Coke. Then Mr. Logan turns his attention to Kevin's problem. "So you don't want to get your father a tie, or socks, or anything ordinary like that, right?"

"Right," Kevin says.

"And he doesn't have hobbies. What's important to him?"

"His job," Kevin says. "And, well . . . me, I guess."

"Hmm . . . do you have a good photo of yourself? Or maybe one of you and your father together?"

Kevin thinks. "Yeah, from when we went fishing last summer."

"Okay, here's the deal. You get that photo blown up to say, five by seven. Then get a nice frame for it, leather if you can afford it."

Kevin considers this. The more he thinks about it, the better he likes it. Something about the way his father's been acting lately tells him this might be the perfect gift. "He can put it on his desk at the station."

Mr. Logan nods. "That's right. Hey, maybe I should start a consulting service. Advise people on their gift purchases." He pretends to be stern. "You're a lucky fellow, Kevin Delaney. You're getting my services for free. Now, who else are you shopping for?"

Kevin fishes the list out of his jacket. "I still have to get something for my aunt, and my buddies, and one more cousin . . ."

"Mother?"

Kevin's head jerks up. He thought Mr. Logan knew. He shakes his head. The waitress arrives with their order. Mr. Logan doesn't pick up his sandwich immediately.

"I'm sorry, Kevin. I know your parents separated, Miss Anthony told me. It wasn't gossip," he adds hastily. "Teachers pass on information like that to each other in case a student is having problems."

"They didn't separate," Kevin tells him. "She left. She just took off."

Mr. Logan picks up his sandwich and takes a bite. He gazes at Kevin with interest as he chews. After he swallows, he remarks, "You make it sound like she ran away from home."

"Well, she did, sort of." Kevin is getting uncomfortable with the direction of this conversation.

"How did this come about?" Mr. Logan asks. His tone is casual, like they're talking about Little League or something. And he isn't bugging Kevin for information. Kevin can just say he'd prefer not to discuss it, and he knows Mr. Logan would accept that, and they could talk about school or something.

But Kevin doesn't say he'd prefer not to discuss it. To his wonderment and horror, he finds himself telling all. He talks about the fighting, the yelling, the tension. He tells Mr. Logan about what he heard and couldn't understand. About coming home one day to find her packing a suitcase.

And Mr. Logan doesn't give him that awful sympathetic look. He speaks matter-of-factly. "Did she tell you why she wanted to leave?"

"It doesn't matter and I wasn't interested anyway." Kevin doesn't bother to disguise his bitterness. He's gone this far, he might as well let it all show. "She wanted me to come with her, but I said no way, *I'm* not deserting my father."

30

"At least you know she still loves you," Mr. Logan says mildly.

Kevin hears his own voice rising. "Who cares? I don't want her to love me. She doesn't love my father, and he's the greatest guy in the world, and if she can't love him, she can't love me either." He has a feeling he's not making much sense, and now he's starting to squirm. He steels himself for some stupid lecture, the kind Mrs. Payne keeps trying to give him, about how he should talk to his mother and try to understand and all that junk.

But all Mr. Logan says is "You must be pretty angry."

Kevin is surprised, and pleased. He hates the way most people think he's supposed to be sorrowful. He's not sad; he's *mad.* And Mr. Logan is the first person to understand this. What an amazing man.

Just then, he sees Andy with his brother Jason. They're coming into the café. Andy spots him and Mr. Logan at the same time, and he looks embarrassed.

Kevin's face starts burning, too. The place is small. There's no way they can pretend not to see each other.

"Hi," Kevin mumbles as they come closer. "Hi, Jason."

Andy's so embarrassed he forgets his manners. He doesn't even greet Mr. Logan. "What are you doing here?" he asks Kevin.

"I saw Mr. Logan at this store, and, uh . . ."

"Hello, Andy," Mr. Logan says pleasantly.

Andy tries to recover. "Hi, Mr. Logan. Um, this is . . ." but before he finishes, Mr. Logan rises and extends his hand.

"Hi, Jason, good to see you."

Jason Rollins shakes hands with him. "How's it going, Jeff?"

Kevin and Andy watch in bewilderment as Mr. Logan indicates the two other chairs at their table. "Have a seat, join us."

"Kevin and I have to go meet Eric," Andy says.

Kevin gets up. "Yeah. See you next week, Mr. Logan. Bye Jason."

The boys beat a hasty retreat. They walk down the mall in silence for a minute.

"Well, now we know Mr. Logan's first name," Kevin says. "Jeff."

"Yeah. What were you talking to him about?" Andy asks.

"What to get my father for Christmas. He gave me an idea." He tells Andy about the framed photograph.

"That's cool," Andy says. He shoves his hands in his jacket pockets. "It's weird, isn't it. Mr. Logan knowing my brother."

Kevin hesitates. "I wonder where they know each other from."

32

Andy looks at him sharply. "You think Mr. Logan's . . . like Jason?"

"I don't know," Kevin says. "I guess he could be." He pauses. "Maybe we shouldn't tell Eric. About Mr. Logan and your brother being friends. You know how Eric is."

Andy nods. "I'm not going to say anything." There's another silence.

"He's still okay, though," Kevin says. "Mr. Logan, I mean."

"Yeah," Andy says. "So's my brother."

Kevin nods. "Right."

CHAPTER
THREE

Kevin has always believed that the first day back at school after Christmas break is the worst day of the year. There are always some decorations left in the classroom, a scrap of tinsel or something, to remind you that what you'd been looking forward to for so long was over. The weather is chilly and gray in January, and the days until spring break seem to stretch out endlessly before you.

They've been back at school for two weeks now, and for Kevin, the gloom hasn't lifted. Miss Anthony is droning on about the battles at Lexington and Concord, and Kevin is only half listening. He'd done his reading in the textbook the night before, and he knows exactly what she's going to say. He's one of the few students who doesn't groan when she announces a pop quiz.

He hears Eric behind him push his desk closer so he can copy off Kevin's paper. His eyes shift to the right, where he sees Emily shoot Eric a reproving look. Kevin catches her eye, and gives her a what-can-I-do-about-it shrug. She smiles sympathetically and shrugs back.

The quiz is easy, and Kevin finishes quickly. But he doesn't want Miss Anthony to think he isn't concerned, so he pretends to study his answers while his mind wanders.

Christmas was OK, not bad at all, considering. There was the usual Christmas Eve dinner at his aunt and uncle's. He spent most of the evening teaching his young cousins how to use a computer game. There was one bad moment when Aunt Louise asked Charley if he'd heard from *her.* But all Charley had to do was give her one good, long look and she dropped the subject.

In the morning, it was just the two of them, but Charley really tried to make it cheerful. He even attempted sausage and biscuits and cheese grits, their traditional Christmas breakfast. It was a disaster, but Kevin appreciated the effort.

And then there were the gifts, especially nice ones this year. Rollerblades, a Gameboy, a watch, and more.

Kevin couldn't remember ever having uncovered such treasures under the tree before. When he thought he couldn't possibly expect anything else, he discovered yet one more package, buried behind the lower limbs of the tree. It wasn't in department store gift wrapping like the others. This package was in brown paper, and there were stamps on it.

He didn't recognize the address in the upper left corner, but there was a name above it. He studied it for a while, finding that if he stared at it long enough, it began to look strange, almost unfamiliar.

He could feel his father's eyes on him. "Aren't you going to open it?"

"No," Kevin replied. "I'm going to send it back."

His father didn't argue. "You can write 'return to sender' on it and leave it for the mailman. That way you don't have to pay postage. Hey, buddy-boy, this photo is really great. It's going on my desk so every cop in Greendale will know what a terrific kid I have."

"Kev, move your hand!" The loud whisper behind him cuts the memory short. Kevin debates pretending he doesn't hear Eric. Luckily, he doesn't have to make a decision.

"Pass your papers forward," Miss Anthony is saying. "It's time for P.E."

This announcement is greeted with mixed reactions. Some kids perk up, a few groan. Winks are exchanged, but also grimaces. Kevin isn't exactly sure how he feels. Just as Eric predicted, health education hasn't been about nutrition. Mr. Logan made that clear on their first day back. Kevin remembers his opening words to the class.

"For the next couple of weeks, we're going to discuss sex. *S-E-X*. It's not a dirty word and it's not a joke. So if you want to laugh, go ahead and do it now and get it out of your system."

They didn't exactly laugh, but there were plenty of muffled giggles. And they didn't get it out of their system.

Mr. Logan has been pretty cool about it. He makes them use the right words for things, like parts of the body, but he seems aware of their discomfort and he's sympathetic. He encourages them to ask questions, and he never ridicules them. Just yesterday, Mary Alice Kinsey, the dumbest girl in class, raised her hand and asked, "Can a girl get pregnant from a toilet seat?"

Kids snickered, and Eddie Lewis yelled out, "Depends on what you're doing on the toilet seat!" Even Kevin, who'd been trying very hard not to laugh, cracked up.

Mr. Logan just smiled. "Actually, Eddie, you're right. If a female has reached puberty, that is, if she has begun to menstruate, she is usually capable of becoming pregnant through sexual intercourse, no matter where the act takes place. But no, Mary Alice, a girl cannot get pregnant from sitting on a toilet seat alone."

Kevin is amazed by the way Mr. Logan can say those words without blushing. If Kevin used words like that in front of his father, Charley would turn red and possibly send Kevin to his room.

Today, Kevin has no idea what to expect in P.E. As the students file out into the hall, and beyond the hearing of Miss Anthony, Eric nudges him.

"Let's ask Mr. Logan if we can talk about boobs."

Emily hears this. "They're called breasts, Eric."

Eric eyes her flat chest meaningfully. "How would *you* know?"

Emily gives him a withering look, and Kevin can't blame her. Eric's been taking advantage of the class and Mr. Logan's good nature, asking silly questions that he already knows the answers to, just to get a reaction from the girls. Kevin suspects that Mr. Logan sees right through him.

Kevin pauses in the hall to let Andy catch up with him. Andy's dragging his feet. "I'll be glad when this is over," he tells Kevin. "Mr. Logan's cool, but all this sex business gives me the creeps. And my parents keep asking me what we're learning about." He shudders. "I'm embarrassed to tell them."

"Some of it's interesting," Kevin comments. "I guess we have to know this stuff. For later, I mean."

"I guess," Andy concedes grudgingly. "What are you doing after school today? Want to come over? I got a new Nintendo game for Christmas."

"Can't," Kevin replies. "I have to go to the hardware store with my father."

They enter the gym and step onto the open bleachers that line one wall. There are no assigned seats for this class, but the girls huddle together at one end while the boys go to the other. The giggling starts even before they sit down.

"Okay, settle down," Mr. Logan says. "We've got some serious material to cover today." He *looks* serious, even more than he has on previous days. "Today, we're talking about a dangerous disease that can be sexually transmitted. How many of you have heard of AIDS?"

Practically everyone raises a hand.

"Good," Mr. Logan says. "Now, how many of you know exactly what AIDS is?"

This time, fewer hands go up, and they go down before the teacher can call on them. Mr. Logan doesn't seem surprised. "The word AIDS is actually an acronym, a word formed from the first letters of other words. The letters stand for Acquired Immune Deficiency Syndrome. What this means is—"

He stops. Larry McCall's got his hand in the air. "Yes, Larry?"

"It's a disease for queers, right?"

Mr. Logan raises his eyebrows. "Queers?"

"You know, fags."

Kevin and Andy make eye contact, then quickly look away. Mr. Logan is gazing at Larry sternly. "Larry, in this class, we use the appropriate and proper names. I presume you're asking if AIDS mainly affects homosexuals, is that correct?"

"Yes, sir," Larry says. "Sorry."

Mr. Logan continues. "In the United States, the majority of the AIDS cases have been homosexual men. But thousands of other people have gotten the disease too. And in some other parts of the world, such as Africa, it has predominantly spread among heterosexuals. The most important thing for you to understand is that *anyone* can get AIDS. Even children."

A murmur goes through the class. Mr. Logan lets it pass before he goes on.

"Let me get back to what AIDS is. AIDS is caused by a virus known as HIV. HIV stands for Human Immunodeficiency Virus. We all get infected by viruses sometimes. Colds, flu, chicken pox, and measles are all pretty common illnesses caused by viruses. Your body has something called an immune system that's like a security force. It can fight these viruses. But HIV is very hard for the body to fight. That's because when the HIV virus gets inside someone's body it destroys some of the person's immune system. Without a strong immune system, the body can't fight HIV or other diseases."

Some of the kids are looking confused, and Mr. Logan sees this.

"Who has a question?"

"So if you have HIV is that the same as having AIDS?" a boy in the back asks.

"No. A person can have HIV but have no AIDS symptoms at all. When a person has HIV *and* they develop certain other infections *then* we say that they have AIDS. There are people who have been infected with HIV for ten years, maybe more, but they have not developed AIDS. With the research that's going on now, there is the possibility that with proper medical treatment, people may be able to live a normal lifetime with HIV and never develop AIDS."

"Can AIDS be cured?" a girl asks.

"No," Mr. Logan says. "There is no cure for AIDS yet. And there's no vaccine, like the one for polio, to protect people from getting it. So we have to learn as much as we can about this disease and we have to protect ourselves."

Mary Alice Kinsey raises her hand. She looks scared. "How do people get this virus?" she asks.

"There are only a few ways," Mr. Logan says. "Luckily HIV can't live in air or in water or on things that infected people touch. That means you won't get

HIV just by being around someone who is infected. You won't get it by shaking hands with them or by sharing a desk or by using the same telephone they did. HIV is only spread through direct contact with body fluids like blood or semen. People have contracted the virus through blood transfusions in the past, but that rarely happens any more since hospitals now test the blood first. Other people who are at risk are drug users who share their needles. But having unprotected sexual relations with someone who is already infected is the most common way HIV is spread. That means sexual intercourse without the use of a condom."

Kevin looks at Andy, and they both roll their eyes. As far as Kevin is concerned, he can hardly bear *talking* to most girls. Forget about touching them.

Mr. Logan goes on to talk about women who can pass the infection to their unborn children, or give it to their babies through breast milk. Kevin finds all this pretty interesting, but some of the kids look bored, and Kevin can understand why. None of this seems to have anything to do with *them.*

Mr. Logan seems to sense their restlessness too. "I'm giving you more information than the Board of Education requires me to," he tells them. "And maybe I'm telling you more than you need to know at your age. I hope I can safely assume that none of you are even thinking about having sex or taking drugs. But I think it's important for you to know what's going on. Right now, there are about one million people in this country who are infected with HIV. There are more than 250,000 diagnosed cases of AIDS."

Someone whistles, and Mr. Logan nods. "Yes. That's a lot of people."

By the time class is finished, Kevin feels overwhelmed. He makes his way slowly down the bleachers, letting others run ahead. He has something he wants to say to Mr. Logan before he leaves.

"Mr. Logan, I wanted to tell you, my father really liked the photo in the fancy frame."

"That's good, Kevin. What did you think of the discussion in class today?"

"Pretty depressing," Kevin says.

"It's a depressing subject," Mr. Logan agrees. "Tomorrow will be more upbeat. We're talking about pregnancy."

Kevin makes a face, and Mr. Logan laughs. "Not too crazy about that subject either, huh? Well, we'll be done with this curriculum in another week. Then we'll be playing volleyball." He cocks his head to one side and eyes Kevin thoughtfully. "Now, what's the matter with *that?*"

Kevin wishes his face wouldn't reveal everything he was feeling. He glances around. No one's within earshot. Even so, he lowers his voice. "I'm too short for volleyball," he confides. "I can't get the ball over the net."

Mr. Logan shakes his head. "You don't need height to play good volleyball. It's a question of power and strength. Building up your arms. Stop by my office one day after school. I'll lend you some weights and show you some exercises."

Kevin thanks him and hurries out to rejoin his class. He's in a much better mood now. Talking to Mr. Logan always seems to do that for him.

After school, he walks outside with Andy, Eric, and Larry McCall. "You sure you can't come over?" Andy asks him. "Larry's coming too."

"No, Dad's probably waiting for me now. He's off today."

"You spend an awful lot of time with your father," Eric remarks. Kevin detects a note of envy in his voice.

"Sure, I like being with him. Besides . . ."

"Besides what?" Eric asks.

"Nothing." He doesn't want to say "besides, my father needs me now." It's too personal.

He sees Emily walking ahead of them. She's with Christie Clark, the most developed girl in the entire sixth grade. The boys are walking more quickly than the girls, and soon they're right behind them.

"Hey, Christie," Eric calls. "How about some safe sex?"

Christie ignores him. That doesn't discourage Eric. "Mr. Logan told us to have safe sex. Don't you always do what teachers tell you to do?"

This comment doesn't get Christie's attention either, but it gets a response from Emily. There's clear annoyance on her face when she turns. "Mr. Logan did not tell us to have any kind of sex. He's teaching us about safe sex so we can be prepared when we're older and ready."

"But I'm ready now!" Eric exclaims. "And look at Christie. She's *definitely* ready!"

Christie turns slightly, and Kevin catches a glimpse of her expression. Her lower lip is trembling. He feels crummy about this. Why does Eric have to act like such a jerk?

"Knock it off, Eric," Andy mutters.

"What's the matter, Christie?" Eric taunts. "Is it that time of the month?"

Kevin knows Emily's expressions. He can see her annoyance turn to fury. She presses her lips together tightly, as if she is afraid of what words might escape if she doesn't. Clutching Christie's arm, she steers her across the street.

"You're a maniac, Fields," Larry murmurs, but that's all any of them has to say about Eric's behavior.

The boys reach the corner where they have to separate.

"See ya," Kevin calls and watches them walk away. He wishes he could go with them. He'd rather hang out with the guys, play some video games or whatever, than tag along with his father to some boring hardware store. But Charley wants his company, and Charley's got dibs on his time.

He doesn't walk too rapidly because he doesn't want to catch up with Emily and Christie. When he opens the door to his house, he calls out, "Dad, I'm home," but only Ms. Tolliver's there.

"Your father got called in to the police station to work the afternoon shift," she tells Kevin.

Kevin groans. Not that he was dying to go to the hardware store. But he could have gone to Andy's with the others. He could still go now, but he doesn't want the guys to know that his father bagged out on him.

He goes upstairs to change his clothes. In his room, he pulls off his sweater and goes to the closet for his favorite old sweat shirt, which used to be his father's till it shrunk in the dryer.

He tries not to look at the package on the closet floor. Why did he put it there anyway? Now he has to see it every time he opens the closet door. He picks it up and shoves it under his bed. Out of sight, out of mind, he hopes.

He doesn't know why he didn't send it back, like he told his father. If his father found it, how would he feel? Kevin knows how he himself would feel. Like a traitor. Well, at least he hasn't opened it. He isn't totally disloyal.

He ambles back downstairs and looks in the refrigerator. He's not hungry, just bored. Finally, he puts his jacket back on, goes outside and across the lawn.

Emily answers the door. "What do *you* want?"

Startled, Kevin steps back. "What's your problem?"

"You're the one with the problem, Kevin," she says.

"What are you talking about?"

Emily's face is grim. "Why did you let that creepy friend of yours say those nasty things to Christie?"

"It's not my fault that Eric's a jerk," Kevin objects.

"You were acting like a jerk, too," Emily accuses him.

"I didn't say anything!"

"Exactly!" Emily declares. "You didn't try to stop him. Not saying anything meant you were going along with him."

Kevin clenches his fists. "He was just kidding, for crying out loud. He was joking around with her. Can't you girls take a joke?"

Emily's voice rises. "Don't you understand that

people can be sensitive about the way they look? Christie has feelings! He wasn't making jokes; he was poking fun at her. He hurt her. Christie's up in my room right now. Crying!"

"Girls," Kevin growls.

"Not girls, Kevin. Human beings. But you don't care, do you? All you care about is yourself and your buddies and trying to be some sort of macho man."

All Kevin can come up with is the line his father used to give his mother to end their arguments. "Give me a break," he mutters and stalks away.

He's had arguments with Emily before. There's a lot they don't agree about. But this one . . . he felt like he was being attacked. And for what? For being loyal to a buddy?

He's mad at Emily. She wasn't fighting fair. All that crap about having no feelings and not caring and being a macho man. Someone else used to throw around words like that. He can remember his father's frustration. Well, now he can understand it. *Frustration* was a good word for what he was feeling.

He starts up the steps to his house, then changes his mind. He doesn't want to hang around the house with Ms. Tolliver. He needs his pals. He walks rapidly, running part of the way, and he's at Andy's in fifteen minutes.

"Hello, Mrs. Rollins."

"Hi, Kevin. The boys are down in the rec room."
Passing the living room, he sees Andy's older brother in there, sitting on the sofa with one of those little computers on his lap. Jason salutes him, and Kevin waves back. Then he runs down to the rec room. The guys are gathered in front of the TV, playing a game.

"Gotcha!" Larry yells. "I win!"

Andy sees Kevin. "Hey, what happened?"

"Dad got called in to the station." He pauses. "I just saw Emily. She says Christie's real upset about what Eric was saying to her."

"Tough," Eric says.

"You really shouldn't say things like that," Andy tells him. Kevin tries to change the subject.

"What's your brother doing here? Doesn't he have a place in Atlanta now?"

"He's doing something for my father," Andy says. Eric's fiddling with the TV and gets a regular program.

It's that dumb show again with the white-haired man. Kevin wonders if he's on TV twenty-four hours a day. "Should we be distributing free condoms in high school?" he asks in his booming voice.

"Turn it off," Larry groans. "I'm sick of hearing about that stuff."

"Sick of what stuff?"

Kevin turns to see Andy's brother coming down

the stairs, carrying his computer. Larry answers Jason's question. "Safe sex. Condoms. AIDS."

Andy explains. "'We're having sex ed. in P.E."

"Oh," Jason says. He puts his computer on a desk and opens it up. "Well, sex ed. is important. You need to know about it. Maybe not for now, but for later, when you're thinking about it."

"*I* don't think it's so important," Eric says. "I mean, having sex is important, sure. But all that AIDS crap, I don't need to hear about that."

Jason looks up from the computer. "Do you know how many people in this country have AIDS?" he asks Eric. "Do you have any idea how many people have died?"

"What are you doing, Jason?" Kevin asks quickly.

"I'm making an inventory of household stuff on the computer, for my parents' insurance," Jason replies, turning away from Eric. "Andy, is there a VCR on that TV?"

Before Andy can answer, Eric is speaking again. "My Uncle Ted says that AIDS is a curse on homosexuals."

Jason looks at him evenly. "Your Uncle Ted is wrong."

Eric shrugs. "Who cares, anyway."

"I care," Jason replies. "And so should you."

"Why?" Eric challenges him. "Nobody I know has AIDS."

50

Jason stares at him for a second. "How do you know that?"

Andy looks at him in alarm. Jason's voice becomes warmer. "No, don't worry, I'm fine."

Eric lets out something between a snort and a laugh. Andy glares at him. "Shut up, Eric."

Now Kevin's very nervous. No one tells Eric to shut up without retaliation. Eric stands up, folds his arms across his chest, and speaks to Jason. "My father says they've got no business wasting time at school teaching us about sex. And he'll really be mad that we spent all day talking about AIDS. It's not like *we're* going to get it. As long as we don't shoot up drugs. Or turn queer." He puts emphasis on that last word.

Kevin can see Jason's jaw tighten. He rises from his chair and faces Eric squarely. "Anyone can get AIDS. But even if you're not at risk, you should still know about it. *People* are dying from this disease. I do volunteer work at a Gay Health Clinic. I see them every day. We all have to care."

"*You* have to care," Eric declares loudly. "I don't!"

"So you don't care about people?" Jason demands.

"I don't care about fags!" Eric yells back.

Jason looks like he wants to haul off and slug Eric. But he only throws up his hands in despair and stalks out of the room.

Andy is pale and shaken, and Kevin doesn't feel

51

so great himself. But Eric is grinning, as if he just won a fight. He saunters over to Jason's computer.

"Don't mess around with that," Andy warns.

"I just want to see if he's got any games," Eric says. He hits a button and studies the menu on the screen. "Network. Isn't that a game?"

"I better get home," Kevin murmurs to Andy, and Andy nods. But just as Kevin is about to put on his jacket, Eric hits another button. He lets out a whoop. "Whoa! Check this out!"

He sounds excited. Kevin and Andy join him at the computer. On the screen is a list of names and addresses. The heading reads HIV Support Network.

"You shouldn't be looking at that," Andy says, sounding frightened. "Turn it off. Now!"

He reaches for the power button to do it himself but Eric pushes his hand away. "Look!" He points to a name on the list.

Jeffrey Logan. 628 Maplewood Drive. Greendale.

There's a phone number too, but Kevin's suddenly feeling so light-headed that the numbers don't register. He recalls seeing Mr. Logan once early in the fall, when he was in a car with his father. Mr. Logan was mowing his lawn. On Maplewood Drive.

"What the hell are you doing?"

They all jump at the sound of Jason's voice. They hadn't even heard him come downstairs. There's no time for anyone to get the file off the screen, and Jason can see what they've been looking at.

He shoves Eric aside, slams the computer closed, and walks off with it. It all happens in a flash. But even in his own shocked state, Kevin doesn't miss the horror and anger on Jason's face.

CHAPTER
FOUR

On Saturday morning, Kevin studies himself in his bedroom mirror as he practices his exercises. With a five-pound weight in each hand, he brings his elbows together, the way Mr. Logan showed him.

That list, on Jason's computer—it must have been a mistake. There is nothing wrong with Mr. Logan. Kevin watched him carefully two days earlier when he demonstrated using the weights to build up biceps. He looked strong and healthy.

"Kevin, are you ready? Let's go!"

"Coming, Dad."

Kevin puts down the weights and pulls on his special bowling T-shirt, with Son of a Cop emblazoned on the back. He runs downstairs, where Charley is waiting with a bowling bag in hand. They go out to the car.

"How are those exercises coming along?" Charley asks him.

Kevin flexes an arm. There's nothing even remotely resembling a muscle there yet, but he's optimistic. "Pretty good, I think."

"Nice of that teacher to lend you the weights," Charley comments. "If you keep it up, I'll buy you a pair."

"Thanks, Dad," Kevin says automatically. Lately, Charley's always offering to buy him things. Kevin has no objection to that. Sometimes, though, he has this odd feeling, like he's being bribed. For what, he's not sure.

At the bowling alley, Kevin goes to the counter to exchange his tennis shoes for bowling shoes. Will is there with a boy who looks to be about Kevin's age.

"Kevin, this is my nephew Kyle from Atlanta," Will says. "He's posing as my son."

The boys exchange greetings and put on their shoes. "Are you a good bowler?" Kyle asks.

"Not bad," Kevin replies modestly.

"I'm terrible," Kyle confesses. "I'm going to make an awful fool of myself."

"Don't worry about it," Kevin tells him. "I'll help you if you want. This is a pretty easygoing bunch. No one gets too serious." They pick out their bowling balls and join the others at their lane.

Eric's there, and Mr. Fields. There are a couple of other cops around with their sons, but those boys are older and Kevin doesn't know them. Eric's trying to strike up conversations with them, so Kevin sticks with Kyle. As each person bowls, he points out to Kyle what the bowler's doing right or wrong.

When it's Kevin's turn, he picks up the ball and goes to the head of the lane. He takes his time to aim. He's just about ready to roll the ball when, behind him, he hears Mr. Fields speak to his father.

"Charley, what do you think about this business with the kids' P.E. teacher?"

Kevin's swing falters. The ball rolls into the gutter. He curses silently, and then turns to Kyle, who's watching curiously. "I wasn't concentrating," Kevin explains. "I took my eyes off the center pin. That's why the ball went off to the side." He speaks loudly and clearly, and the sound of his voice drowns out the conversation between his father and Mr. Fields. But he knows what's coming.

"Kevin," his father calls. "Why didn't you tell me about this?"

"About what?" Kevin asks, stalling for time. "Wait a second, Dad." His ball's back, and he picks it up for his second shot. This time, he aims properly, but he only manages to knock down a few pins.

"Kevin," Charley calls again.

He can't put it off any longer. He ambles over to his father and Mr. Fields.

"Is this true?" Charley asks. "That teacher, Logan . . . he's got AIDS?"

He wishes his father wasn't looking at him so intensely. He would like to take a moment to give Eric a seriously dirty look. Was Eric nuts, blabbing about this to his father? And since when are he and his dad so chummy?

"Dad, I don't think Mr. Logan has AIDS. His name was on this list about HIV, but maybe it's just because he's interested in helping people or something."

Mr. Fields is paying no attention to Kevin's explanation. "Jeez, this is exactly what the kids need," he mutters. "A fag gym teacher." He grins suddenly. Then he puts one hand on his hip and holds the other hand out, with a dangling wrist. He begins mincing around, jerking his hips back and forth. In a high-pitched, shrill voice, he says, "All right, boys, let me see some push-ups. Ooh!"

"He's not like that," Kevin protests, but the other cops are watching and laughing, and no one hears him. Eric is practically doubled over.

At least Charley doesn't laugh. "It's nothing to joke about," he barks. "This guy teaches *physical education*. There's a lot of touching that goes on."

Mr. Fields grabs Eric by the arm. "This Logan ever touch you?" he asks.

"No . . . I mean, he has to, in gymnastics, but . . ."

Mr. Fields isn't grinning anymore. "I don't want some fag touching my kid."

Charley's expression is grim. "I don't want anyone with AIDS touching mine."

Kevin tugs at his father's sleeve. "Dad, I told you, he doesn't have AIDS."

Eric cuts in. "What are you, a doctor?" He's speaking to Kevin, but he's looking up at his father expectantly.

Kevin keeps talking, very fast, trying to get it all out before he loses his nerve. "Besides, even if he did have AIDS or HIV, you can't get it from someone touching you. You can only get it from blood or, you know, something like that."

Charley's not angry at Kevin for arguing, but there's a deep crease running along his forehead. "Phys. ed. can get rough, Kev. I've seen blood on a gym floor."

Will's nephew Kyle has been listening. "There was a kid at my school two years ago who had AIDS," he offers. "They made him leave."

"My wife was talking about a PTA meeting this week," Mr. Fields says to Charley. "Maybe we should go."

Charley's eyebrows go up. "To a PTA meeting?"

"Sure, I don't trust the ladies to look into this. We need to check out this Logan character, find out if it's true. And what the school system's going to do about it."

"Hey, Charley," Will yells. "You're up."

Charley glances back at Mr. Fields, nods shortly, and goes to the lane.

A couple of hours later, in the car on the way home, Charley is quiet.

"Dad, are you really going to that PTA meeting? You never went to one before."

"There's never been any need before," his father replies. "Parents've got to look out for their kids, Kev. I'm the only parent you've got." He grins suddenly. "But they better not try to get me involved in one of those cake sales!"

An image of pecan pies crosses Kevin's mind, and he speaks before he even considers what he's saying. "Dad . . . do you ever think about her?"

"No." He takes his eyes off the road just long enough to give Kevin a sharp look. "Why? You been talking to her?"

"No! I was just wondering . . . what she's doing and all that."

"What do you care?" Charley demands to know. "Hey, don't forget, she walked out on us, buddy-boy. She's history." He speaks evenly, unemotionally, but there's an undercurrent that tells Kevin his curiosity is out of line. He tells himself he won't bring up the subject again.

"I'm on duty till eleven tonight," Charley tells him. "You going over to the Paynes'?"

"No," Kevin says. His eyes slide over to his father. Charley looks pleased.

Kevin hasn't made up with Emily. For the past couple of days they haven't spoken. Her mean, un-called-for words still burn in his ears. He can't believe she hasn't gotten over that dumb business. *Girls*. And he thought she was different.

Still, it's lonely in the house that night. He calls Andy. "You want to come over?"

"I can't," Andy says. "My brother's coming over for dinner. He's bringing . . . company." He speaks guardedly, and Kevin suspects he's not alone in the room.

"Oh," Kevin murmurs. He's guessing that "company" means a boyfriend. It's weird. But he supposes Jason's lucky that he's got parents who don't mind him bringing this boyfriend home to dinner.

"Andy, do you think it's true? About Mr. Logan?"

There's a silence at the other end of the line. Kevin can hear voices in the background. Then they fade away.

"I had to wait till my parents went out of the

room," Andy says in a low voice. "Yeah, I think it's true. Because Jason called me the next day, and he said we shouldn't tell anyone what we saw on that computer file."

Kevin's heart sinks. "Eric—"

"What about Eric?"

"He told his father."

There's a sharp intake of breath on the other end. Then Andy speaks, dully. "I have to go now. My brother's here."

Hanging up, Kevin is restless. He doesn't want to think about Mr. Logan or Eric or what's going to happen. He goes up to his room, thinking he might read, but he's aware of the package under his bed and someone else he doesn't want to think about. So he goes back downstairs and turns on the television. Fiddling with the remote control, he finds a movie and settles back on the couch to watch.

But it's a boring movie, and Kevin can't get interested in it. His eyelids are heavy, his whole body feels heavy, and he lies down on the couch.

When he opens his eyes, the TV is blaring the theme music for the news. He's amazed to see that it's eleven o'clock. His father should be home in just a few minutes. Bleary-eyed, he gazes at the screen.

"A night of horror and near tragedy for a family on Desmond Drive in Greendale," the newswoman intones. With effort, Kevin hoists himself up on his elbows. The main story on the news was never about Greendale.

"The Culver family, including two young children, were held hostage for three hours by an armed man recently released on parole, who broke into their house at around seven-fifteen this evening. The assailant apparently believed that the Culver family had a fortune hidden somewhere in their house."

On the screen appears a distraught woman, her hair in disarray. "He was crazy!" she sobs. "He told us we had until midnight to produce a million dollars in cash. If we didn't, he said he'd kill us all!"

The newswoman is back. "Around ten o'clock, the older Culver child, eight-year-old Megan, managed to leave the dining room where the family was being held. She got to a phone and dialed 911. The gunman discovered her before she could speak, and ripped the telephone cord from the wall. Fortunately, the 911 operator traced the call and reported the broken connection over the police radio. A nearby patrol car picked up the message."

Kevin's wide awake now. He stares in disbelief at his father on television.

"I went to the house to investigate," Charley says. "And I detected suspicious activity through a window. I entered through another window in the back of the house and apprehended the suspect."

An off-screen voice asks, "Why didn't you call for backup?"

Charley replies, "In assessing the situation, I determined that danger to the family was imminent and decided that immediate action was called for."

He vanishes, and it's the newswoman's face on the screen again. "A struggle ensued between Officer Delaney and the assailant. Officer Delaney was able to disarm the assailant, and miraculously, there were no injuries. The Culvers are calling Officer Delaney a brave and daring hero.

"In Atlanta today, the governor announced . . ."

The governor could be announcing the end of the world as far as Kevin is concerned. He leaps off the couch, and then he just stands there, shaking all over. His legs feel so wobbly, he's not sure if they'll keep him upright. But then the phone rings, and his legs come through for him.

"Hello?" he says, surprised to find his voice sounding so normal.

"Hey, man, it's Eric! I just saw the news!"

"Yeah, me, too."

"My dad's standing right here. He wants to speak to your father."

"He's not back yet," Kevin tells him. "Wait, there's the door. Maybe that's him now." He drops the phone and runs, dimly aware of the fact that his father wouldn't be ringing his own doorbell.

He peers through the peephole. Mr. and Mrs. Payne are on the porch. It's not until he opens the door that he sees Emily behind them.

"Kevin, we just saw the news," Mr. Payne says. "Is your father back? Have you heard from him?"

"No, sir. Uh, come in, I guess he'll be back soon."

Emily is wide-eyed. "Your father's going to be famous! I can't believe he did that!"

Kevin remembers Eric on the phone. He races back, but Eric has hung up. No sooner does he replace the receiver than the phone rings again.

This time it's Will. "Holy smokes, Kev! Your old man's a hero! Congratulations! Tell him to give me a call when he gets in, OK?"

The phone doesn't stop ringing. Other cops, a few friends from school, friends of his father . . . He tries to keep a list. Emily joins him in the kitchen. "This is incredible," she says between calls. "I know things like this go on all the time in Atlanta, but nothing like this has ever happened in Greendale!"

"I know," Kevin says, hanging up the phone for what he hopes is the last time.

"And he did it all by himself," Emily marvels.

Now Kevin is actually feeling kindly toward her. "That's my Dad. He's not afraid of anything."

"He could have been hurt," Emily notes.

"Yeah, well, he wasn't."

"Kevin, here comes your father now," Mrs. Payne

calls from the living room. Kevin runs to the door. He's not sure what to expect.

Charley walks in, looking more tired than he's ever seemed to Kevin. But his arms open to his son, and Kevin rushes into them. Charley holds him unusually close for a moment.

He greets the Paynes with more warmth than he has in recent months. He shakes hands with Mr. Payne, and Mrs. Payne gives him a brief hug.

"Thanks for coming over," he tells them. "I was trying to get back here, but between the captain and the newspeople—" he shakes his head wearily—"I could use a drink. How about you folks? Kevin, why don't you get a soda for you and Emily?"

"You've had quite an ordeal," Mr. Payne remarks.

"I'll bet the captain wants to give you a medal," Kevin says on his way to the kitchen. He grabs two cans of Coke from the refrigerator. On his return, he hears Mrs. Payne saying, "But wasn't that reckless, going in that house alone? How could you put yourself in such danger?"

Charley shrugs as he hands her a drink. "I didn't have much choice. The guy was a madman. There was no telling what he'd do to that family."

"And you," Mrs. Payne murmurs.

Charley shrugs again. "That's the risk you take when you're a cop."

Mr. Payne rises and goes to the window. "But don't

you usually try to minimize those risks? Isn't that the normal procedure?"

Kevin's eyes dart back and forth between the Paynes. What's the matter with these people? They should be congratulating his father, praising him, slapping him on the back, not asking stupid questions. He just rescued a family, for crying out loud!

Charley gulps his drink, then sets it down. "You do what you have to do," he says flatly.

Mr. Payne turns to his wife. "We should be going. It's way past Emily's bedtime."

Mrs. Payne nods. "We just wanted to make sure Kevin wasn't upset."

"Everything's fine," Charley says. He walks them to the door. Emily lags behind.

"Were you scared?" she asks Kevin.

"Scared of what?"

"Your father can get killed doing things like that."

"Shut up," Kevin says fiercely.

"Sorry," Emily says. She hurries out with her father. Only Mrs. Payne lingers in the doorway. She speaks softly to Kevin's father.

"Charley, going into that house . . . it was suicidal." Charley says nothing, but that doesn't stop her. "I know you're in pain. But you've got Kevin to think of."

Charley still doesn't respond to her words, and his

face offers no reaction. Only Kevin sees the white knuckles on his clenched fist. When he does speak, his voice is low. "Good night, Laura."

"Dad?"

Charley closes the door and turns.

"What was she talking about?"

"She thinks I should have waited for backup before I went into the house. It would have been safer."

"But you were able to save those people all by yourself! You didn't *need* backup."

Charley goes back to the liquor cabinet and pours another drink. A sudden tingle of fear passes through Kevin. Could his father have died in that house? Of course he could have. But that was what a hero would do—risk death to rescue others.

The phone rings. Charley doesn't move.

"I'll get it," Kevin says. He goes to the kitchen.

"Hello?"

"Kevin, it's Mom."

He freezes.

"Kevin? Are you there?"

"I'm here."

"I just heard about your father. Is he all right?"

"Yes."

"Is he there with you?"

"Yes."

"Let me speak to him, darling."

He lays the phone down on the counter, and goes back to the living room. "Dad? It's . . . her. Mom. She wants to talk to you."

He's in the process of refilling his glass. He doesn't speak. Kevin waits a few seconds and then returns to the phone.

"He can't talk to you now."

Her voice becomes urgent. "Kevin, I have to see you. I know you don't want to talk about this, but we must. I want you to understand—"

He cuts her off. "I have to go, too."

"Kevin! I love you!"

He hangs up the phone.

CHAPTER
FIVE

Over the next couple of days, Kevin is swept up in the wake of his father's glory. On Sunday, Will and two cops come over, and it's like a party. Will presents Kevin with a gift. It's a specially made T-shirt, like his bowling one, but with one difference. The back reads Son of a Hero.

"Wear it to school Monday," Will suggests. "Let everyone know who you are." Kevin thanks him, but he doesn't think he'll wear it to school. The kids would think he was showing off.

He discovers on Monday that he doesn't need a T-shirt to proclaim his new status. Everyone knows what his father did. And they treat Kevin almost like *he's* the hero, just for having such a brave father.

"Hey, is your father really Batman in disguise?" Eddie Lewis jokes, but his eyes are full of admiration. Another guy has brought the Sunday newspaper article about the incident. "Can you ask your father to autograph this for me?"

At lunch, there aren't enough chairs at his table for all the kids who want to sit with him. From other tables, goofy girls keep sneaking peeks at him and offering smiles. But that doesn't give him half the thrill as when Parker Davis, the biggest jock of the sixth grade, approaches him. "A bunch of us are hanging out at the Y this afternoon to shoot some baskets. Want to come?"

He's never had such respect before from his classmates. Even Eric is in awe. "My father says he doesn't know any other cop who would have the guts to do that. Except him, of course."

Kevin can't quite picture the overweight, slow-moving Mr. Fields apprehending a dangerous criminal on his own. But he's kind. He can tell Eric's a little jealous.

In front of the whole class, Miss Anthony says, "Your father has to be a special person, Kevin. I know that you're very proud of what he's done."

"Yes, ma'am," Kevin says. There should be a stronger word than proud for what he's feeling.

Walking down the hall to the gym, he notices kids from other classes, people he doesn't even know, pointing at him. Even the principal speaks to him. "That's quite a role model you have, young man."

All the excitement has kept him from thinking about Mr. Logan. But in the locker room, changing into his gym shorts, he hears one guy saying to another, "Man, I'm glad we're done with all that sex and AIDS stuff." Now it's in the front of his mind again, and he dreads seeing Mr. Logan.

But Mr. Logan isn't in the gym. Students wander around aimlessly, and Kevin joins his buddies. "Just our luck," Andy grumbles. "Today we start volleyball and Mr. Logan's absent. Why couldn't he have been absent last week? Then we wouldn't have had to listen to all that stuff about having babies."

"I wonder if he's sick," Kevin says nervously.

Eric's grin is wicked. "Maybe the principal found out about you-know-what and fired him."

Kevin stiffens. He wants to come up with a great retort, but nothing comes to mind. As it turns out, that's not necessary. To his immense relief, Mr. Logan comes running in, looking undisturbed and healthy. Only his smile is strange. It goes up one side of his face. And when he speaks, it's out of one side of his mouth.

"Sorry, kids," he announces. "Dental emergency.

Okay, I've divided you into two teams, but you have to elect your own captains."

Kevin's good humor is restored. His spirits reach new heights when he's unanimously voted a team captain. Still, he tries not to feel too excited. There's no telling how long this new popularity will last.

When he gets home that afternoon, he's surprised to find his father there instead of Ms. Tolliver. Charley's sitting at the kitchen table, drinking coffee and rapidly turning the pages of a newspaper. His face lights up when he sees Kevin come in. "Hey, buddy-boy."

"I thought you were on three to eleven today," Kevin says.

"The captain called this morning, told me not to come in. I guess he figures I need a day off."

"You deserve a holiday," Kevin tells him.

Charley grunts. "I've been sitting around all day doing nothing. I don't call that a holiday. Hey, what do you say, let's go over to the sporting goods store and take a look at some weights."

Kevin hesitates. He was planning to go over to the Y and shoot baskets with Parker and his friends. But his father looks so expectant . . . "Sure, Dad. I'll just go change."

When he returns, his father is on the phone. "Right, eight o'clock tomorrow night. I'll pick you folks up at a quarter of." He hangs up, takes a pencil, and makes a notation on the wall calendar. "PTA, 8:00."

Kevin's stomach starts to churn. He'd forgotten about that. Resolutely, he forces it out of his head again.

"You know, Dad, you don't have to buy me weights," Kevin says as they get into the truck. "Mr. Logan says I can borrow his for as long as I want."

"I don't think that's a good idea," Charley says.

"Why?"

"Because it's not a good idea to take favors from him. I don't want you obligated to this guy."

Kevin looks at him in alarm. "Dad! You don't even know him!"

But his father is gunning the motor and doesn't seem to have heard him.

The next morning, Kevin arrives at school early. His footsteps echo in the empty hallway. They make a lonely sound, and it's hard to believe that in just about twenty minutes, these same halls will be crowded and noisy.

His arms ache from holding the bag that contains the weights. He would have waited until after school to return them, but the guys might have tagged along. He prefers to see Mr. Logan alone.

He passes the gym and goes directly to the office just beyond it. The door is ajar, but he raps anyway.

"Come in," Mr. Logan calls, his back to the door. He swivels around in his chair as Kevin enters. "Hi, Kevin, what can I do for you?"

"I just came to return these," Kevin says. He takes the weights out of the bag and places them on Mr. Logan's desk.

"Tired of weight training?" Mr. Logan asks.

"Oh, no," Kevin assures him. "My dad bought me a pair yesterday."

"I've been hearing a lot about your father," Mr. Logan says. "Did he know that guy was armed when he went in the house alone?"

Kevin nods, and Mr. Logan lets out a low whistle. "He's a daring man."

"Yes," Kevin says. "I'll bet he gets a medal for this."

"It must be frightening for you," Mr. Logan muses. "Knowing the kind of dangers your father encounters in his work."

To anyone else, Kevin would deny this, but to Mr. Logan he admits, "Sometimes."

Mr. Logan crumples a wad of paper and tosses it across the room. It lands cleanly in the wastebasket. "Two points," he says. "Do you ever hear from your mother, Kevin?"

Here we go again, Kevin thinks. Kevin knows that all he has to say now is no, and Mr. Logan will drop the subject. But this is the one person who makes him feel like it's OK to talk about her.

"She calls sometimes. But I don't talk to her."

"Why not?"

He remembers his father's words. "She walked out on us! She's gone; she's history. I don't have anything to say to her."

Mr. Logan speaks gently. "She left your father, Kevin, not you."

"It's the same thing," Kevin mutters.

"You know, you might want to hear her side of the story one of these days. You might understand—"

"No, I won't." As he speaks, he's aware that he's interrupting a teacher, something he would never normally do. But Mr. Logan doesn't rebuke him. "I'll never understand," Kevin says.

"Maybe not," Mr. Logan concedes. "Sometimes it's impossible to understand why people do what they do. But you have to try."

"It wouldn't change anything," Kevin argues.

He's startled to hear Mr. Logan say, "You're probably right." He rises and begins straightening papers on his desk. "Kevin, one of the things we learn as we get older is that there's a lot we can't change about our lives. We can't control everything that happens to us. There are some things that are just out of our hands."

"What's the point of talking to her then?" Kevin asks.

Mr. Logan smiles slightly. "Because even if we can't change what happens, or understand, at least we can learn to accept. We accept, we cope, we make the best of it."

Kevin isn't exactly sure what he's talking about. But he likes the way Mr. Logan says *we,* not *you.* Like they're in this together. Like he's got problems, too.

He wishes he could ask straight out, "Are you sick?" But you don't talk to teachers about things like that. And maybe he doesn't want to know.

"I guess I'd better get to class," he says reluctantly.

"See you in the gym," Mr. Logan says. He salutes and adds, "Captain."

Kevin goes to the door, pauses, and he turns back. "Mr. Logan . . ."

"Yes?" He's got a notebook in his hand, and he's looking at it.

"Do all teachers go to the PTA meetings?"

"Most of them."

"Are you going tonight?"

Mr. Logan nods.

It takes a lot of self-control not to say "don't go." But Kevin manages.

"You want to hang out at the Fieldses' tonight?"

Kevin looks up from his homework. "What, Dad?"

"I'm picking up the Fieldses," Charley says. "Their car is in the shop. If you want, you can stay there with Eric while I'm at the PTA meeting, and then I'll get you when I bring them back home."

"OK," Kevin says. The notion of spending an evening with Eric doesn't exactly thrill him. But it's better than being alone without anyone to distract him from wondering what was going on at the meeting.

In the car, Kevin watches his father anxiously as he drives. There's a set, determined expression on his father's face that makes him uneasy. "Dad," he says slowly, "you know, Mr. Logan is real nice. He's an awfully good teacher."

"I'm sure he is," Charley says. "But you're my responsibility, Kevin. Mine alone. I have to know what's happening at that school." A brief smile appears. "Don't worry, son. I won't embarrass you."

Kevin can't imagine Charley Delaney embarrassing anyone. That's not his worry at all.

When they arrive at the Fieldses', he's glad to see that he won't be alone with Eric. Andy's there, too. The grown-ups take off for their meeting, and the boys sprawl on the living-room floor to watch the basketball game on TV.

"Man, I wish I could be at that PTA meeting," Eric remarks.

"Why?" Kevin asks.

"My dad's going to make a major fuss," Eric announces with pride. "And let me tell you, my dad knows how to make a fuss."

Kevin sits up. "What kind of a fuss? What's he going to do?"

"He's going to let the school know that Mr. Logan has AIDS, and he's going to demand that they do something about it."

Andy chews on a fingernail. "But your father doesn't know if Mr. Logan *does* have AIDS. That list said HIV, remember? We don't even know for sure if he's got *that*."

Eric shrugs. "It's easy enough to find out. Ask your brother."

"That won't do any good," Andy replies. "I know Jason wouldn't tell me."

"Yeah, I guess fags stick together," Eric says. "Anyway, even if he doesn't have AIDS . . ." He stops speaking. Andy's face is turning crimson.

"Don't call my brother a fag."

Kevin can't remember the last time he saw Andy look so angry, or heard him speak so strongly.

"Well, he *is* one, isn't he?" Eric counters.

"He's gay," Andy says. "He's a homosexual. You wouldn't call a black person a nigger, would you?"

Kevin suspects that Eric just might do that, but at least he'd have to know it's wrong. Still, Eric's not giving in.

"That's not the same thing," he says. "A black person can't help being what he is, he's born that way. It's different for fags. Oh, excuse me, I mean, homosexuals." He exaggerates each syllable of the word.

"You don't know that's true," Andy argues. "There are some scientists who think a person can be born gay."

"How do you know so much about it?" Eric asks. "You in training, or something?"

"Knock it off, Eric," Kevin says helplessly. He knows his words won't have any impact. Any second now the two boys will be slugging it out.

But Andy doesn't rise to Eric's needling. "I know a lot because . . . well, because Jason talks about it. He gave me and my parents stuff to read."

"Gross," Eric mutters, but Kevin is intrigued. Andy's never really talked about Jason before. Now that the subject is out in the open, there's something Kevin has always wondered.

"Andy, how did Jason get to be gay? I know it's none of my business," he adds hastily. "But I'm just curious."

"Why?" Eric interjects. "You want to take lessons?" He laughs at his own stupid humor. Kevin doesn't acknowledge the question, and Andy ignores Eric, too.

"He says he knew he was different from other guys when he was in high school," Andy tells him. "Like, he went out with girls, but he never, you know . . ."

"Wanted to get their clothes off?" Eric suggests with a smirk.

Andy suddenly becomes intent on relacing his high tops, but he keeps talking. "Yeah, I guess. Anyway, the summer before his senior year, he had a job up in South Carolina, as a lifeguard. He met this other lifeguard who was gay, and they got to be . . . friends."

Eric starts making loud gagging sounds. What Andy's saying doesn't appeal to Kevin, either, but it occurs to him that Andy's got guts.

"So, he wasn't born gay," Kevin says.

"I don't know," Andy replies. "Jason says it doesn't matter how people get to be gay."

"Can we stop talking about this?" Eric asks. "You're making me sick."

But Andy continues. "He says all that matters is for people to accept themselves for what they are, and for other people to accept them and not hate them. Or try to change them."

This is all sounding very familiar to Kevin. He recalls his conversation that morning with Mr. Logan.

Eric crawls forward to the TV and turns it up. The noise drowns out the possibility of more conversation. That's actually OK with Kevin. What Andy's telling them is interesting. But it's making him think about what might be happening to Mr. Logan right that minute.

Luckily, it's an exciting basketball game, and Kevin gets caught up in it. The timing is perfect, too. The clock runs out just as the glare of headlights appears through the living-room windows.

"They're back," Kevin says, unnecessarily. He jumps up and goes to the window. It seems like ages pass before his father and the others come into the house.

Andy's parents are with him as well as the Fieldses. None of them look very happy.

"How about some coffee?" Mrs. Fields asks. She disappears into the kitchen.

"What happened, Dad?" Eric asks eagerly.

Mr. Fields sinks down heavily into an armchair. "I can't believe they already knew about him."

Kevin's heart sinks. "Knew what?" he asks, even though he knows the answer. He looks at his father, but Charley is standing with his back to Kevin, staring out the window at nothing.

Mr. Fields is speaking to the other adults, but what he says confirms Kevin's fear. "It's incredible! They know this guy's got a contagious disease, a *killer* disease, and they let him teach!"

Kevin's heart sinks, and Andy asks the question. "Does Mr. Logan have AIDS?"

His mother puts her hand on his shoulder. "He's HIV positive, Andy. He has the virus, but he doesn't have AIDS."

Kevin edges over to his father and looks up at him inquiringly. His father's still staring out the window, but he responds. "It seems Logan told the school board about his diagnosis in October. But that's not grounds for dismissal, your principal said, being HIV positive."

"I don't give a damn what they call it," Mr. Fields barks. "He's got no business being around kids."

Mrs. Fields returns with coffee and begins serving it. Mr. Fields takes a noisy slurp. "Not to mention the fact that he's a fag."

Kevin glances at Andy. He knows Andy wouldn't correct an adult.

But someone else does. Mr. Rollins speaks with dignity. "Please don't use that word, Carl."

Mr. Fields just grunts.

"So he's not going to be fired," Kevin says in relief.

"The school's not going to do a damn thing," Mr. Fields states. "So we're going to have to."

Mrs. Fields is twisting a ring on her finger and eyeing her husband nervously.

"I want this guy out of the school system," Mr. Fields continues.

"Can't you just leave him alone?" Kevin bursts out.

"Kevin!" His father says warningly.

"I'm sorry, sir," Kevin mumbles to Mr. Fields. But Mr. Fields isn't paying any attention to him.

"It's up to us to get rid of Logan," he says.

"We're not in any position to do that," Charley replies.

"Then we're going to get in position. We'll get people behind us, stir up a real stink. Believe me, once the taxpayers put some pressure on the school board, they'll listen." Mr. Fields's voice rises with each word, and his face is taking on a purplish tint.

"Carl, *please*," Mrs. Fields whispers.

Mr. Rollins looks like he's trying to control his temper. He speaks through tight lips. "Take it easy. I'm sure the school board wouldn't put the kids in a dangerous situation. If they thinks it's OK—"

"Well, it's not OK with me," Mr. Fields retorts. "And I guarantee you, it's not going to be OK with other parents once they start thinking about it."

Mrs. Rollins clears her throat. "David, I think we'd better be going. Get your jacket, Andy."

All the Rollinses move toward the door. Mr. Fields rises and follows them. "Do we have your support?"

Mr. Rollins speaks calmly. "I'm sorry, Carl. No."

Mr. Fields practically slams the door behind them. "It figures. Their older kid's a queer, right?"

"He's gay," Kevin murmurs. "Homosexual."

No one is paying attention to him, not even his father. "Exactly what are you planning to do?" Charley asks Mr. Fields.

"I'm no good at making speeches," Mr. Fields says.

He flashes a grin. "You know what the captain says about my interpersonal relations. What we need is a leader, a spokesman, someone everybody looks up to. Somebody people will listen to."

"You got anyone in mind?" Charley asks.

"Yeah. You."

Kevin clutches his father's arm. "Dad, you *hate* making speeches. Remember when you had to make one at that retirement party?"

Charley tousles his son's hair. "You're right. I don't know, Carl. I don't think I'm the right man."

"What are you talking about, you're perfect!" Mr. Fields insists. "People *like* you, they respect you. Especially now. The whole town knows your name." He strides over to Charley and stands so close to him that Kevin thinks his father must feel the man's breath. "You can't just stand by and let this go on. You owe it to the community. You owe it to Kevin."

He turns suddenly, grabs Kevin's arm, and thrusts him forward. Kevin winces from the pressure of Mr. Fields's grip.

"Look at your kid!" Mr. Fields demands. "You want him to die of AIDS? You're willing to risk your life to save strangers. What about your own son?"

Charley bows his head toward Kevin. He looks at him, long and hard.

"Dad—" Kevin says urgently.

"I'm not going to let anything happen to you," Charley says. "You're all I've got." He looks up at Mr. Fields.

"I'll think about it."

CHAPTER SIX

Kevin knows that news travels fast in Greendale. Still, it's something of a shock to arrive at school the next morning and find everyone talking about Mr. Logan.

In their classroom, before Miss Anthony shows up, the students form their usual clusters, girls on one side, boys on the other. But as he wanders around the room, Kevin hears the same topic of conversation in each group.

"I can't believe it," Larry McCall is saying. "He doesn't *look* sick."

"You better believe it," Parker Davis declares. "My

mother says he admitted it right in front of everyone at the PTA."

Kevin passes a girls' group. Mary Alice Kinsey is very upset. "When we were doing gymnastics, he held my legs on the balance beam!" she wails.

"You can't get HIV from touching," Emily says. "Weren't you listening when he talked about it in class?"

"Well, of course he's going to say that," pipes up another girl. "He wants to keep his job."

In another group, Eddie Lewis is holding court. "You know how he's always coming into the locker room when we're getting dressed? Now we know why."

Kevin had planned to stay out of the discussion, but this comment is so ridiculous he can't ignore it. "He comes in the locker room because we always start horsing around and making noise."

"That's what *you* think," Eddie declares. His eyes narrow suspiciously. "Hey, wasn't he giving you extra help after school last month? You were *alone* with him." He gives the other guys a meaningful look.

Eric comes to Kevin's defense. "Watch it, Lewis, don't mess with Kevin. I know something about him you don't know." He pauses to build up some suspense. "His father's going to get Mr. Logan fired."

Everyone's expression changes. Now all the guys are looking at Kevin with respect. "Yeah? How?" Eddie asks with sincere interest.

"He said he'd *think* about it," Kevin mumbles. He sees Andy sitting alone in his seat, writing intently. Kevin goes to join him.

Andy's only doodling in the margin of his notebook. He doesn't look up as Kevin perches on the chair beside him, but he speaks. "I wish they wouldn't talk about him like this. It's like everyone's ganging up on him, or something."

"Maybe it'll all blow over," Kevin says, but his words sound hollow.

Miss Anthony comes in, and the students scurry to their seats. Hands go up.

"Yes, Lori?"

"Miss Anthony, did you go to the PTA meeting last night?"

The other hands go down, and everyone watches the teacher expectantly.

"Yes, I was at the PTA meeting." She hesitates and looks torn. "I know you've all been hearing stories about what went on, but the teachers have been asked not to permit discussion in class. But please talk to your parents about this, OK? Don't rely on rumors. Now, open your math books to page 182." It's clear that they're not going to get any information out of her.

She keeps them very busy that morning, and she watches them like a hawk. Even in the cafeteria at lunch, she moves around from table to table, effectively preventing any real discussion of Mr. Logan.

But when it's time for P.E., she lets them loose, and the hall buzzes with predictions.

"Do you think he'll say anything?" Christie Clark asks.

"I'll bet he just pretends nothing happened," Parker declares.

"I'm guessing he won't show up," Eric states. "He won't have the guts to face us."

Eric's wrong. Mr. Logan is waiting for them in the gym when the boys and girls come out of their locker rooms. Some of the kids start taking their positions around the volleyball net, but Mr. Logan stops them.

"Everyone, go sit on the bleachers. I want to talk to you for a minute."

Once they're seated, he stands before them with his arms folded across his chest. "I'm sure you've all heard stories and rumors about what went on at the PTA meeting last night. You're entitled to know the true story, and I'd like you to hear it from me. Then, if you have any questions, I'll answer them." He pauses.

"He's so calm," Andy whispers to Kevin.

Kevin marvels at that, too. *His* heart is pounding furiously. But Mr. Logan seems totally in control.

"I do not have AIDS," Mr. Logan states. "A few months ago, I had a blood test, and I was diagnosed as being HIV positive. As you'll recall from our discussion, this means I have the virus which can cause AIDS. Right now, I have none of the symptoms of AIDS, and the virus hasn't affected my energy. Now, I know a lot of you may be worried that you can catch this virus from me. Does anyone remember how you can catch the AIDS virus?"

Several hands go up, and Mr. Logan calls on Emily.

"You can catch it from having sex or sharing a needle with someone who is infected. Or from a contaminated blood transfusion."

"That's right," Mr. Logan says. "So you cannot catch this virus from me. Any questions?"

In front of Kevin, Eric turns around. "I'm going to ask how *he* caught it."

"Don't," Kevin hisses.

"How are you going to stop me?" Eric challenges.

Kevin thinks frantically. "I'll never let you copy off my tests again."

"Whose side are you on, anyway?" Eric grumbles. But he doesn't raise his hand. Only one person does, a girl sitting on the bottom row.

"Yes, Angela?"

"How do you feel?" she asks.

Mr. Logan smiles, a deep, broad, reassuring smile. "I feel fine. And hopefully, I'll be feeling fine for a long, long time. OK, folks, let's play volleyball."

Kevin is relieved. He's eager to tell his father what Mr. Logan said. Surely, once Charley realizes that there isn't any danger, he'll drop this whole business.

When he gets home that afternoon, his father's out. Ms. Tolliver's downstairs doing laundry. She says Charley went to the grocery store and he'll be right back. Kevin heads to the kitchen, makes himself a bologna sandwich, and sits down at the table.

He sees a neatly typed letter lying there, and he glances at it curiously as he eats his sandwich. Certain words catch his eye. He puts the sandwich down, wipes his hands on a napkin, and picks up the letter. His eyes widen as he reads.

"To the editor: At this week's meeting of the West Greendale Elementary School Parent Teacher Association, parents received some disturbing news. The school physical education teacher, Mr. Jeffrey Logan, has the AIDS virus. When asked what the school intends to do about this, Principal Robert Fisher declared that no action would be taken. As a parent, I believe that this is outrageous and irresponsible on the part of the school. Schools are supposed to provide our children with a safe and secure environment in which they can learn without the threat of contracting a serious disease. Certainly, I sympathize with the plight of Mr. Logan. But my child is my primary concern, and I am sure all other parents feel the same. For the protection of our children, it is imperative that the school board terminate the employment of Mr. Logan."

The letter is signed Charles M. Delaney.

Kevin has to read it again. He can't believe his father wrote this. It doesn't even sound like him. He never used words like *imperative* or *terminate*. And who was this editor person it was written to?

He hears the door open, and then his father appears in the kitchen. He's carrying a large grocery bag.

"What's that?" Kevin asks. "I thought we were going grocery shopping tomorrow."

"This is for tonight," Charley says. "I've got some people coming over, and I figured I'd better get some refreshments for them."

Kevin watches as his father begins pulling out boxes of doughnuts and cookies. All Charley ever provided his buddies with before was potato chips and beer.

Kevin's still clutching the letter, and he holds it up. "Dad, what's this? I wasn't snooping," he says quickly. "I didn't mean to read it, but it was just lying here on the table."

His father's not annoyed with him. "That's OK. You'll see it in the newspaper tomorrow anyway."

"The newspaper," Kevin echoes.

"Yeah, that's just a copy. I dropped it off at the newspaper on my way home this afternoon. What do you think of it? Pretty fancy writing, huh?"

"Yeah. It doesn't sound like you."

Charley grins. "I had some help from a lady at the station who used to be an English teacher."

"Dad, . . . Mr. Logan talked to us in class today. He says he's feeling fine and we can't catch anything from him."

"Well, what else is he going to say?" He pulls a can of coffee and a box of tea bags from the shopping bag.

"How many people are coming over tonight?" Kevin asks.

"Don't know for sure. It's a meeting of parents. I've been calling people all day. So has Mrs. Fields, and a couple of other people. I think we've managed to reach every parent in town."

"Oh." Kevin doesn't have to ask why the parents are meeting. "When did you have time to make all these calls?"

"I've got plenty of time these days," Charley mutters. "They've got me on desk duty."

"Desk duty! Why?"

Charley shrugs. He takes the letter from Kevin, folds it, and sticks it in a drawer. "This will be the second time in a month your old man's name will be in the paper. What do you think of that, buddy-boy?"

"Neat," Kevin murmurs. "Dad, can I go next door tonight and do homework with Emily?"

Charley frowns slightly, but he says, "Yeah, OK. It might get kind of noisy here."

"Are her parents coming to your meeting?"

"No."

They've just finished dinner that evening when parents start arriving. Kevin stays in the kitchen to do the dishes. When he comes into the living room, he counts at least thirty people there. And they all seem to be talking at once.

Kevin gets his books, slips out, and runs across the lawn. Emily opens the door.

"Hi, c'mon in." She peers out at the line of cars parked in front of Kevin's house. "What's going on at your place?"

"My dad's having a meeting," Kevin says, walking in. "Hi, Mrs. Payne."

"Hello, Kevin."

"Do you know about my father's meeting tonight?"

"Yes," she replies. But she returns to the sofa and picks up her book.

Emily and Kevin go into the dining room and spread out their homework.

"What's the meeting for?" Emily asks.

"It's about Mr. Logan. My father thinks he shouldn't be teaching anymore."

"Didn't you tell him what Mr. Logan said today?"

"Yeah. I guess he doesn't believe it."

"Wait a minute." Emily leaves the room. When

she returns, she's carrying a pamphlet. She tosses it on the table. "Tell your father to read this."

Kevin looks at the title: "What You Need to Know about AIDS." He pushes it away. "He's not going to read this."

"Doesn't he want to know the facts?" Emily asks. "*My* parents do."

Her tone is annoying him. "My father knows what he's doing. He's not stupid."

"I didn't call him stupid," Emily replies patiently. "But if he knew the facts about AIDS, he'd see that he doesn't have to be afraid of someone who's infected."

"My father's not afraid!"

"Then why does he want Mr. Logan to stop teaching? Why is he making such a fuss?"

Kevin glares at her. He won't let *anyone* criticize his father. But there's no point in arguing with her. Emily's like a dog with a bone, she won't let go of something once she's got her teeth in it. He can't walk out, he'd have no place to go but home. So he forces his anger to the back of his mind and opens the social studies textbook. "Which of these questions are we supposed to answer?"

Emily looks like she wants to say more but thinks better of it. They get to work on their homework. Kevin keeps an eye on the cars parked out front. As soon as most of them are gone, he gathers up his books. "See ya tomorrow," he says.

When he gets home, Eric's parents are still there, and some woman Kevin doesn't know.

"This is a good start," the woman is saying. "I'll have the flyers made up tomorrow and start distributing them."

"Fine," Charley says. "Did you get a copy of the petition?"

"Right here," she says, patting her handbag.

"Dear, do you think we really need a demonstration at the school?" Mrs. Fields asks her husband.

"It's worth a shot," Mr. Fields replies. "Anything that makes a noise is OK with me."

"I wouldn't count on much of a turnout," Charley says. "People aren't going to miss work to march in front of the school."

"They will if the school doesn't take action pretty soon," Mr. Fields replies.

The guests leave, and Charley begins straightening up. "You want a doughnut, Kev?"

"OK. How was your meeting?"

"Fine."

Kevin follows him into the kitchen. "Dad, are there really going to be demonstrations?"

"Kevin, none of this concerns you."

"Dad, he's *my* teacher!" Kevin blurts out.

Charley slams the door of the cupboard so hard

Kevin almost drops the books he's still holding. "Now listen up, son. I know you like this teacher of yours. But that's got nothing to do with anything. You're going to have to let the adults handle this. You stay out of it, you hear me?"

Kevin shifts the books from one arm to the other. As he does, something falls out from one of them. Kevin picks it up.

It's Emily's pamphlet. She must have slipped it in a book when he wasn't looking.

"What's that?" his father asks. He takes it out of Kevin's hand and examines the cover. "You don't need to be reading this," he says with a grimace. He drops it in the wastebasket.

"Dad! It's not mine, it belongs to Emily."

"Figures. Go to bed, Kevin."

"Yes, sir." He makes a mental note to fish out the pamphlet in the morning.

Waking, Kevin can hear his father downstairs. But he doesn't jump out of bed to join him. He lies there, staring up at the ceiling, hoping this isn't a garbage collection day.

As soon as he hears the front door slam, he gets up. He washes and dresses and goes downstairs. He retrieves Emily's pamphlet from the garbage and flaps it in the air, trying to rid it of the smell of onions.

The morning newspaper is on the table. His father has left it open at "Letters to the Editor."

Kevin puts the pamphlet down and reads Charley's letter again. It looks very official and important printed in the newspaper. There are a couple of other letters, too, all about Mr. Logan, all of them agreeing with his father.

Kevin wonders if Mr. Logan reads the morning paper. He shivers. How awful it must be to know that so many people want to get rid of you.

He glances at the clock. He'll have to eat fast if he's going to make it to school on time. But since he's not the least bit hungry, it doesn't matter. He collects his books, puts on his jacket, and heads out.

When he gets to school, he sees a large group of kids in the parking lot. They all seem to be watching something. Kevin edges through the crowd so he can get a look.

At least it's not much of a demonstration, just five women and one man carrying signs. Each sign is different, but they all say pretty much the same thing.

He tries to imagine Mr. Logan arriving at school, to be greeted by these people yelling "No AIDS in school." Did he get upset? Did he walk past them and pretend they weren't there? Or did he get back into his car and drive away?

No, not the last. He can't picture Mr. Logan running away. He's not that kind of person.

Mr. Fisher, the principal, comes out the main door. He looks nervous, but he speaks in his usual booming voice. "Sorry, folks, but I'm going to have to ask you to move on. You don't want to disrupt your kids' education, do you?"

The adults stand around uncertainly for a moment, talking among themselves. Kevin can't hear them, but he watches their expressions. Most are reluctantly nodding. Then they move slowly toward their cars.

When Kevin goes into his room, Emily corners him. "I saw your father's letter."

That figures, Kevin thinks. She's probably the only kid in class who reads the newspaper every morning. "So?"

Emily doesn't beat around the bush. "That was a terrible thing to do!"

Eric and a couple of other guys are watching. Kevin meets Emily's eyes. "My father's got a right to have an opinion. It's a free country, you know!" That's a pretty lame response, but it's the best he can come up with.

The morning passes slowly, and Kevin finds it hard to concentrate. He keeps seeing Mr. Logan reading the newspaper, seeing Charley's name, recognizing it. He dreads facing the teacher in P.E.

When Miss Anthony announces that it's time for P.E., he doesn't notice all the hands going up right away. Eric speaks first. "I've got a note from my parents excusing me from P.E."

"Are you sick?" Miss Anthony asks.

Eric's tone is cocky. "No, and I don't want to be. That's why my parents say I don't have to take P.E. as long as Mr. Logan's teaching it."

"I have a note, too," another student calls out.

"So do I."

"Me, too."

Altogether, there are seven students who have notes. Miss Anthony looks disturbed, almost like she's about to cry.

"It's certainly your parents' right to take you out of a class, but I wish . . ." She stops and pulls herself together. "All right. Those of you who are not going to P.E. can spend the period in the library."

Kevin almost wishes he had a note so he wouldn't have to face Mr. Logan. On the way to the gym, Andy walks alongside him. "Bunch of jerks," Andy says. "I never heard of anyone getting AIDS from playing volleyball." He pauses. "My father said your father had a letter in the newspaper."

"Yeah." Then Kevin adds, "It's not like I can tell my father what to do."

Andy nods, and Kevin can see that he understands. After all, Andy knows Kevin's father; he knows how stubborn Charley can be. But Mr. Logan doesn't know this. All he'll know is that Kevin Delaney's father wants him fired.

But either Mr. Logan didn't see the letter, or he doesn't care. He greets them all with his easy smile, though his brow puckers a bit when he sees how many are missing. He calls Kevin and Parker, the other volleyball captain, over to him.

"You guys are going to have to rearrange your teams today," he says. "With so many kids absent, the sides won't be even."

That's all he has to say on the subject of the missing students. Parker's team has more members missing than Kevin's so Kevin gives him some players.

Despite the reduced team sizes, they have an excellent game. Everyone has to move quickly to make up for the gaps on the floor, and the ball flies back and forth more rapidly and frequently. With fewer kids on each side, each player has more opportunities to take a whack at the ball. Kevin discovers that he *has* developed a more powerful serve, and he rarely hits the net.

More than before, the kids are really into the game. It's fast and noisy and everyone has a major part to play. Mr. Logan runs around them, calling out instructions, offering tips, cheering them on.

By the time the period is over, everyone's in a good mood. Mr. Logan sends them off to the locker rooms with a cheery "great game!"

"That was cool," Larry McCall tells Kevin. "Maybe I shouldn't say this, 'cause I know Eric's your buddy, but it's a better game when he's not here. He hogs the ball."

Everyone in the locker room is in high spirits. No one even mentions Mr. Logan. It's almost enough to make Kevin believe things are going to get back to normal.

Until he goes home. When he walks in the door, he's completely unprepared for his father's greeting.

"What the hell is this doing here?"

Kevin's stomach plunges when he sees what his father is holding. Emily's pamphlet. He'd left it on the kitchen table.

Charley's not waiting for Kevin's response. "When I put something in the garbage, it's because it belongs there, and it's supposed to stay there!"

"I was going to give it back to Emily," Kevin stammers but his father isn't listening.

"I don't want you reading this crap, you understand?"

"It's not crap," Kevin begins.

"Don't talk back to me!"

"Just look at the cover," Kevin pleads. "It's written by a doctor."

"I don't give a damn who wrote it," Charley rages. "Doctors don't know everything about this AIDS thing!'' With his massive, strong hands, he rips it in half.

"Dad!'' Kevin wails.

Charley is breathing hard. He seems to be making an effort to get his temper under control. "Now, listen to me, boy, this is the last time I'm going to say this. You stay out of this business. I'm in charge of getting rid of this Logan character, and I won't have my own son running around defending him. You want to embarrass me?''

Kevin's trying very hard not to cry. "I'm the one who's going to be embarrassed! I have to see Mr. Logan every day.''

"Not anymore you won't. I'm taking you out of P.E.'' Charley rips a piece of paper from the pad by the telephone, sits down at the table, and begins to scrawl.

"Dad, don't! Please!''

The pain in his voice must have penetrated Charley's anger. For a moment, he stops writing and rubs his forehead. When he speaks again, his voice is a little calmer. "Kevin, I can't let anything happen to you. If there's one chance in a million you could get that disease——''

"But there isn't,'' Kevin says eagerly. He joins his father at the table.

His father continues as if he hasn't spoken. "You

sweat in the gym, right? You're playing volleyball. Logan's sweating, he throws the ball to you. The sweat gets into your skin."

"You can't get it from sweat," Kevin begins, but his father is shaking his head.

"You don't know that."

There's something in his eyes Kevin has never seen before. It's not anger anymore. It's something he can't quite identify.

Charley rises. "I have to go to a meeting."

Kevin remains at the kitchen table after he's left. The remnants of the pamphlet lie there, a grim reminder of his father's outburst.

He notices that there's a light blinking on the telephone answering machine. His father must have been so furious when he saw the pamphlet that he forgot to listen to his messages.

Kevin hits the playback button. There's a beep, and then a soft, sweet voice.

"Kevin, darling, I hope you get this message before your father erases it."

He reaches out to hit Stop, but his hand hovers in midair.

"I know he doesn't want you to talk to me, and you don't want to do anything he disapproves of. But someday, you will want to let me be your mother again. And I just want to let you know I'll always be here, waiting."

There's another beep, and no more messages. Kevin gets his books and starts upstairs.

He can't help wondering what she'd have to say about Mr. Logan. She'd probably argue with his father. Charley would yell at her, just like he'd yelled at Kevin. And he'd order her to do as he said. Just like he used to, all the time, whenever she dared disagree with him.

In his room, he lies down on his bed. Waves of loneliness pass over him. He's frightened—by who or what, he's not sure.

Then he sits up. *That's* what he saw in his father's eyes—fear.

He moves his head back and forth, as if to shake the idea out of his mind. No, he was wrong, that couldn't be it at all. Charley Delaney wasn't afraid of anything.

CHAPTER
SEVEN

By the end of the week, Kevin's almost glad he's not going to P.E. anymore. The fuss over Mr. Logan hasn't blown over, it's blown up. It's as if half the town has gone crazy. There was no way Mr. Logan could still be ignoring it. And Kevin would just as soon not see the man's reaction.

His father's back on the three to eleven shift, which is fine as far as Kevin is concerned. This means Charley sleeps late in the morning so Kevin doesn't have to see him for breakfast, and he's usually not home until Kevin's gone to bed.

On this particular Friday morning, Kevin is eating his cereal when he hears Charley moving around upstairs. He hastily gulps his orange juice and gets out of the house. Never before has he wanted to avoid seeing his father. It's a creepy feeling. But his father's been acting even stranger than he did just after his mother left. Kevin's afraid to say anything around him, which means he's better off keeping away.

He knows there will be a demonstration going on at school when he arrives. People have been there with signs every day this week. The principal can't tell them to go away anymore. Charley Delaney used his pull to get some special permit that allows the demonstrators to be there. Each day, there have been a few more parents than the day before.

He can hear the chanting a block away from the school. It's louder today. When the school comes into view, he catches his breath. He didn't think the demonstration would have grown *this* much.

There have to be at least fifty people there, chanting, marching. Looking *mean*. Some little kids stand nearby, gaping at them. A teacher comes out from the building and hustles the children inside.

It's still early, so there aren't too many other students around in the parking lot. Kevin sees Emily, sitting alone on the school steps, watching the demonstrators with a sad expression. He goes over there.

"Hi."

She looks up, shading her eyes from the sun. "Hi, Kevin." She moves over to make room for him. Kevin does a quick survey to make sure none of the guys are around to see this. Then he sits down.

He pulls his jacket closer against the cold. "When are they going to quit doing this?"

"Not until the school board fires Mr. Logan," she says sadly. "Isn't it horrible? They're *grown-ups.* They're supposed to be smarter."

Kevin has no answer for that. Grown-ups have been surprising him more and more lately.

"I saw your father on TV last night," Emily says.

"So did I," Kevin replies. For the second time in a month, Charley Delaney had been featured on the news. This time, Kevin was prepared.

He was eating Ms. Tolliver's meat loaf when the phone rang. "It's your friend Eric," the housekeeper said, handing him the phone.

"My father just called from the station and said we should watch the six o'clock news on channel four. And he told me to let you know too."

It was just about six o'clock then. Kevin took his meat loaf into the living room and switched on the TV. He sat through some crime reports, but none occurred in Greendale. Then there was something about the state budget, the threat of a phone strike, a train derailment. . . . Kevin was beginning to think Eric had made a mistake.

"In Greendale today, a school board meeting was

disrupted when angry parents demanded the dismissal of an elementary school teacher."

And there on the screen was Mr. Logan, coming out of a house, glancing toward the camera without any expression and then moving out of range.

"Physical education teacher Mr. Jeffrey Logan has been in the center of a controversy in Greendale since admitting that he carries the AIDS virus."

The scene switched to a packed auditorium. On the stage, sitting behind a table, a man rapped a gavel while people in the audience jeered and shouted insults. Kevin recognized Mr. Fields right away. His face was a fiery red, and he was shaking his fist in the air.

"You've got no business risking the lives of our kids!" he screamed.

Then the camera zoomed in on Charley Delaney.

"Why, there's your daddy!" Ms. Tolliver exclaimed. Kevin hadn't even realized she'd come into the living room.

Charley's name was on the screen, too, just like the last time. But he looked different. He wasn't in uniform, and if Kevin didn't know better, he'd think his father was nervous.

"We don't want to hurt this teacher," Charley said. "We, um, just want to make sure our kids are OK."

An off-camera voice asked, "Do you think this teacher poses a threat to students?"

"Well, nobody knows that much about AIDS, do they? I mean, we can't take any chances. . . ." His eyes were darting back and forth, like a caged animal, trapped and confused. It wasn't an image Kevin liked associating with his father.

"Look, here he comes!"

Still lost in his memory, for a second Kevin thinks Emily is talking about Charley. Then he realizes she's referring to Mr. Logan.

The teacher is getting out of his car. He has a briefcase in one hand, and with the other he locks the car door.

The demonstrators see him too, and they start holding their signs higher and chanting louder.

Mr. Logan doesn't even flinch. He holds his head up and strides across the parking lot. His gaze is straight forward, steadfast. Like a soldier, Kevin thinks.

Mr. Logan passes them on the steps, not pausing, but flashing a smile in their direction.

"He can still smile at us, with all this going on," Emily says in wonderment. "What a brave man."

"He smiled at you, not me," Kevin tells her. "He's got to know that my father's the one who's stirring everyone up."

"Your father, not you," Emily says.

"Same thing." Kevin sees some of the guys approaching, and he rises. "Guess we better get to class."

The door to their classroom is open, and Kevin can hear Eric's shrill voice before they even walk in.

"My dad said your parents won't even sign the petition!" He's yelling. "What's the matter with them anyway?"

"Oh no," Emily moans. They stand in the doorway and see Andy in a corner. Eric is practically nose to nose with him. Andy's pale, but he responds quickly.

"My parents won't sign the petition because they don't think there's any reason to fire Mr. Logan."

"Yeah, right," Eric snarls. "I guess they don't care if you get AIDS. Hey, maybe you already have it. You probably caught it from your brother."

"My brother doesn't have AIDS," Andy snaps.

"Okay, maybe not now, but he's going to get it. You know, my father says maybe AIDS isn't such a bad thing. It'll get rid of all the fags."

Kevin rushes forward and steps between them. "Shut up, Eric! Leave him alone."

"You standing up for him?" Eric asks.

"Yeah, I'm standing up for him. You don't know anything about this."

The light of a new discovery hits Eric's eyes. "I get it! You and Andy . . ." He starts making smooching noises.

A couple of students start laughing. The others just watch apprehensively.

Kevin clenches his fists. "You've got a dirty mind, Eric."

"Yeah, well, at least it's not a fag's mind."

Andy's fist seems to come out from nowhere. It makes contact with Eric's chin. Eric staggers backward, but he recovers quickly. He lurches forward, but Kevin kicks out a leg and trips him. There's a squeal from one of the students.

Eric is so stunned, he remains sprawled on the floor. Miss Anthony walks in.

"What's going on in here?" she asks sharply.

Eric gets up. "I tripped," he mutters.

"Well, take your seat."

Passing Kevin, Eric hisses, "Just wait till your father hears about this."

Kevin knows he'll tell. He doesn't know which will anger his father more—tripping Eric or standing up for Andy.

At lunchtime, Kevin picks up his tray and then hesitates. He can't go to his usual table where Eric is sitting with some other guys. He joins Andy, who's sitting alone at another table.

"Don't eat the sandwich, it's pimento cheese," Andy says.

"OK."

For a few moments, they eat in silence.

"Can I sit with you?"

The boys look at Emily, and then at each other.

Kevin doesn't know if he can handle another shock today. The separation of sexes in the cafeteria is practically a commandment at school.

Well, what did it matter, everything else in his world had been turned upside down.

"Yeah, I guess," Kevin says, less than graciously.

"OK with me," Andy mumbles.

Emily sits and opens her lunch box. "I've got homemade cookies."

Kevin perks up. Sometimes, breaking rules can pay off. Emily hands out the cookies.

"What's that?" Andy asks, pointing to a foil wrapped package in her lunch box.

"More cookies, for Mr. Logan. My mother made them specially for him. He had some at our house yesterday, and he carried on about how great they are."

"What was Mr. Logan doing at your house?" Kevin asks.

"Having dinner. My father thinks he should know that *some* parents support him. They said if the school board fires him, they're going to start their own demonstrations."

"Tell them to call my parents," Andy says. "They'll help out."

Kevin shifts uncomfortably and stirs his soup. "I don't think those people are going to keep on demonstrating. They'll get sick of it."

"It's not just the demonstrations," Emily tells them.

"Mr. Logan's been getting lots of letters and phone calls. Really nasty ones."

"From who?" Andy asks.

Emily makes a face. "They don't sign them; they're too chicken. Mostly, they threaten him. They say if he doesn't leave town, he'll be in serious trouble."

Kevin shivers. "Is he scared?"

"He doesn't *act* scared," Emily says. "He says he only feels sorry for these people. He says they're victims of their own ignorance."

Kevin's head jerks up. Basically, she's calling his father ignorant. He should say something, defend him, stand up for him. But he can't think of anything to say.

"I feel sorry for Mr. Logan," he manages.

"Don't," Emily says. "You don't have to feel sorry for him, *he's* not a victim. He just has some enemies, but he's not letting them get him down. He's standing up for himself."

So's my father, Kevin says to himself, but he doesn't say that out loud. He doesn't think they'll understand. He's not sure he does himself.

"I'm asking some kids to come over to my place after school today," Emily continues. "I think kids should start getting involved in this and let Mr. Logan know we care what happens. Christie's coming and Larry and some other kids. You guys want to come?"

"Yeah, I'll come," Andy says.

"What about you, Kevin?" Emily asks.

He wants to. And he could probably get away with it, too. His father won't be home till eleven.

Then he's stricken with guilt over his own thoughts. How could he even consider being so disloyal?

"I better not," he says to his soup. "I've got a lot of stuff to do."

When Miss Anthony dismisses them that afternoon, he dawdles in the classroom, to let the gang going over to Emily's have a head start. But they're still on the steps when he emerges from the building.

Andy turns to him. "Look," he says, pointing to Mr. Logan's car.

Kevin gasps. Mr. Logan's tires have been slashed, and the windows are shattered. "What happened? Who did this?"

"We don't know," Emily says.

Kevin looks down the row of teachers' cars. No one else's has been damaged. "Does Mr. Logan know about this?"

"Yeah," Larry says. "He's in the office now, calling a garage to pick it up."

"Did he call the police?" Kevin asks.

Christie looks at him through squinty, accusing eyes. "I don't think so. The police probably wouldn't care anyway."

"That's crazy!" Kevin exclaims. "I mean, if there's a crime, it doesn't matter who it happens to, they'll still try to catch the person who did it."

"Maybe *you* should let the police know," Emily says mildly. "At least, you've got connections . . ."

"Maybe I will," Kevin replies. He squares his shoulders and faces them all directly. "You tell Mr. Logan I'm going to the police station right now to report it." He marches down the steps and walks away.

How dare they think the police wouldn't do anything, he thinks. Demonstrations are one thing, but violence is something else. There's no way his father is going to let something like this go on.

The police station is only a few blocks away. The officer on duty in the reception area recognizes him. "Hey, you're Delaney's kid, right?"

"Yes, sir, I'm Kevin. Can you get a message to my father?"

"You can give it to him yourself." He jerks his head toward a door.

Kevin's surprised. "He's still on desk duty?"

The officer grins. "Well, we all need a break now and then, right?"

Kevin moves through the swinging doors. He passes the bulletin board, with its photos of wanted criminals and missing children, without a glance. He takes no notice of the uniformed woman escorting the man in handcuffs, or the table laden with doughnuts and coffee, or the photographer taking a picture of some guy who's just been arrested.

He pauses as he nears the end of the row of desks. His father's back is to him. He's hunched over in his seat, pecking on a typewriter, one letter at a time.

"Dad?"

He swivels around. "Kevin! What are you doing here?" He makes an effort to smile, but it barely creases his face.

Kevin's own smile doesn't rest easy on *his* face, either. "I came to report a crime."

"Oh yeah?" Charley picks up a pad. "Some punk spray graffiti on the school again?"

"No." He takes a deep breath. There's no reason to be nervous; it *is* a genuine crime. "Someone slashed a teacher's tires at school. Smashed the windows, too."

"What teacher," Charley says, and there's no sound of a question mark at the end of the words, like he already knows.

"Mr. Logan."

"Has he called it in?"

"I don't know. He . . . he's been getting anonymous letters, too. And phone calls. People are threatening him."

"Cranks," Charley murmurs. Then he frowns. "How did you find out about the letters and phone calls? You're not going to P.E., are you?"

Kevin shakes his head. "Emily told me. Her parents are friends of Mr. Logan's."

His lips tighten. "I don't want you hanging around at the Paynes' anymore."

"I wasn't at the Paynes'. Emily told me at school."

"Well, I don't want you talking to her at school!" His voice has risen, and a cop glances in their direction. "I'm not even sure I want you going to that school anymore."

Some man sticks his head out of an office. "Hey, Charley, come here and give me a hand with these files. They're all out of order."

His father winces. But he gets up and goes to the office.

Kevin stands there for a minute, watching him. There's a droop to Charley's shoulders he's never noticed before.

"Hi, Kev. What's up?" Will's there, and at least *his* smile is real. To his horror, Kevin feels his eyes starting to well up.

Will puts a hand on his shoulder. "I was just going to have some coffee and a doughnut. How about keeping me company?"

Kevin allows himself to be steered into an empty interrogation room. He's working hard at keeping the tears from being released.

"Haven't seen you in a while," Will says. "We've missed you at the bowling alley."

"Dad's been real busy." There's something he wants to know, but he's afraid it would be like talking about his father behind his back. Luckily, Will brings up the subject.

"Yeah, and your old man hasn't been in the best of moods lately."

Kevin nods fervently, and Will goes on.

"I can't blame him. Between that mess at your school, and being stuck on desk duty . . ."

Kevin breaks in. "Why is he still on desk duty?"

Will hesitates. "Well, it was that hostage incident. The captain thought he shouldn't have stormed that house."

"But he was a hero!" Kevin protests.

"Absolutely," Will assures him. "But the captain thought it was reckless, not calling and waiting for backup. It wasn't a by-the-book police procedure, and the captain's a stickler for the rules. So, he reassigned your father for a while."

"I guess he's not going to get a medal, then," Kevin says.

"No."

Kevin rises and goes to the door. His father's not back at his desk. "Will, tell my father I went on home, OK?"

"Sure." Will follows him out. "Kevin . . ."

He turns.

"Your father's a great guy. He's just had some lousy

breaks lately. That can bring a guy down, you know? Make him feel desperate."

"I know," Kevin says. He wishes Will was his brother, his uncle, some member of his family. So he could *really* talk to him, pour out all the feelings that have become a crazy, churning weight.

He leaves the station. "Desperate," he says aloud as he walks. It was a good word. "I feel desperate." A passing couple glances at him oddly, but he doesn't care.

At home, he can hear Ms. Tolliver vacuuming upstairs. He goes directly to the kitchen. He looks at the telephone for what seems like a long time. Then he picks up the receiver, and hits 411.

"Information, what city, please?"

"Atlanta."

"Go ahead, please."

"Um, can I have the number for Marie Delaney?" The address on the Christmas package is imprinted in his head. "She's on Briarcliff Road."

There's a brief silence, and then a mechanical voice intones, "The number is . . ."

He writes it down. "Thank you," he says, even though he knows that it's just a machine and not a person on the other end.

He sits down at the kitchen table and stares at the piece of paper. Just a bunch of numbers, that's all they were. But if he punched them in on the phone, something would happen. Fifty miles away, a phone would be ringing, and she might answer, and then—what?

He looks at the numbers so long, they're committed to memory. No, he can't do this to his father. Charley Delaney has suffered enough. Dumped by his wife, caught up in a messy controversy, worried about a disease, confined to desk duty—and here was his son, about to betray him.

He crumples the paper and tosses it toward the wastebasket. "Two points," he says aloud as it goes in.

He runs upstairs, waves to Ms. Tolliver, and goes to his bedroom, closing the door to block out the noise of the vacuum cleaner. Getting down on his hands and knees, he fishes around under his bed and pulls out the package, still in its brown wrapping.

Cradling it in his arms, he wonders, would this, too, be an act of betrayal? His father would never know. But *he* would.

"Desperate," he whispers. He rips off the brown paper, very fast, before he can have second thoughts.

It looks like a book, but there's no title on it. The cover is fabric, a deep blue-and-green plaid. Opening it, he sees only blank, lined pages. But an envelope falls out. There's a card inside.

"My darling Kevin," he reads. "I keep a journal and I write in it every night. Sometimes it helps to write about what's happening in your life. I hope you'll use this book to express your feelings, your hopes and dreams. Someday, if you want, I hope we can share our journals. Love, Mom."

It has a nice smell, a fresh new-book scent. What would his father say about this gift? Diaries are for girls, maybe. It doesn't matter.

He sits down at his desk and opens it to the first page. Taking a pen, he chews on it for a second. He writes: "I feel desperate."

Seeing the word on paper makes it even more real. It's easy then to let all the other words come pouring out.

CHAPTER EIGHT

Kevin used to love weekends. He always tried to get his homework done right away on Fridays, so he could enjoy the weekend completely, without anything hanging over his head. Weekends were movies and miniature golf and bowling and junk food. Weekends were never long enough.

But on Monday morning, Kevin feels like he's just been through the longest weekend of his life, and he's glad it's over. Before he goes downstairs, he takes a few minutes to write in his journal.

"Nothing terrible happened this weekend. Nothing happened at all."

He writes about how his father is like a ghost again,

wandering in and out of rooms, sitting in front of the TV like a zombie, forgetting to eat. People called, mostly to talk about Mr. Logan, and even then he sounded listless, not very interested.

"I guess that's good in a way. Maybe all the fuss is dying down, and things can get back to normal." Then he sighs. He doesn't even know what normal is supposed to be anymore.

He closes the book and slips it under his bed. He hates leaving it behind when he goes out. It seems like wherever he goes, he's always thinking about what he'd be writing in it if he had it with him.

Downstairs, he sees that his father left the morning newspaper on the kitchen table. He can't miss the headline: "School Board Refuses to Fire HIV Teacher." His spirits rise when he thinks of Mr. Logan winning. Which, of course, means his father losing. His spirits waver, then plummet, even faster than they rose. He doesn't even know how he's supposed to feel anymore.

It's clear to him how the demonstrators feel about the school-board decision. They're still there at school, in greater numbers. They're louder, too. And they stay longer, even after school starts.

"Class, turn to page 82," Miss Anthony says. Kevin *thinks* she said 82. He can't be sure because the noise outside muffles her voice.

A girl raises her hand and asks a question. Miss

Anthony puts a hand to her ear. "I can't hear you, Mary Alice, you'll have to speak up." She looks in despair at the windows. They're already closed, so there's nothing she can do.

All morning, she has to practically shout to be heard. When Parker goes to the pencil sharpener by the windows, he lets out a whoop. "Hey, the TV people are here."

Several kids make a dash to the window, despite Miss Anthony yelling, "Stay in your seats!" To Kevin, she looks like she's about to cry. Kevin wonders if Mr. Logan can hear the demonstrators in the gym.

If he didn't hear them on Monday, he would have had to hear them on Tuesday. The demonstrators have bullhorns. Kevin wonders if they were provided by the police department.

In the cafeteria at lunch, Andy and Larry are passing around a petition. "Emily made it," Andy tells Kevin. "It says, 'We, the students at West Greendale Elementary School, support Mr. Logan.' " Under that sentence are lines on which the students are supposed to sign their names.

"You want to sign it?" Larry asks.

Kevin swallows, hard. Just then, Eric swaggers over to their table. "What's that?" He snatches up the petition and reads it. Then he tears it in half.

"Hey, what do you think you're doing?" Andy cries in outrage.

"Don't worry," Larry says, "I've got more in my desk."

"I'll take care of those, too," Eric says.

Suddenly, they're all on the floor, right in front of everyone and Miss Anthony, too. "Stop it at once!" Miss Anthony cries out.

Mr. Logan walks into the cafeteria. He sees the fight and hurries over. "OK, break it up," he says. He grabs Eric with one hand and Andy with the other and pulls them up.

"Get your hands off me!" Eric shrieks. Mr. Logan releases him, but Eric doesn't stop screaming. "He touched me! I'm going to tell my father!"

Miss Anthony and Mr. Logan talk in whispers. Miss Anthony orders the boys back to the classroom, and Mr. Logan leaves the cafeteria. It doesn't seem to bother him that everyone's watching him in shocked silence.

On Wednesday morning, the demonstrators are still there. But not for long. Just as Kevin reaches the steps, the principal comes out the front door and stands at the top of them. "Could I have your attention, please?"

Maybe the demonstrators don't know who he is, or maybe they've forgotten how you're supposed to obey the principal. In any case, they keep right on yelling.

But Mr. Fisher has a whistle, and he blows it, hard.

That silences the group for a moment. Kevin thinks the principal looks upset, and he soon learns why.

"You have no reason to be here anymore," Mr. Fisher announces. "It saddens me to tell you that Mr. Logan has resigned. He is no longer a member of our faculty."

The crowd looks like they don't know how to react to this. A few let out a cheer, but it doesn't carry much power. There's a low rumble of conversation, and then they begin to disperse.

Kevin is stunned. He scans the area wildly, looking for somebody, anybody, who might know what this is all about. He spots Emily, dragging her feet as she climbs the steps. He knows he's not supposed to talk to her, but for the first time in his life, he completely disregards his father's orders.

"Emily, wait!"

She pauses at the top of the steps while he takes them two at a time. "What happened?" he asks breathlessly. "Was he fired?"

"No," Emily says. "Didn't you hear what Mr. Fisher said? He resigned."

"*Why?*"

"I don't know. I guess maybe he got tired of it all."

Kevin stares at her in disbelief. Then the realization hits him, and he feels sick. "He gave up."

Emily shrugs and walks on inside the building.

Kevin can't move. He stands there, while classmates brush past him, still trying to grasp this. He remembers watching Mr. Logan stride past the demonstrators, thinking he looked like a fearless, conquering hero.

It was all an act, a pose. Well, maybe that's what adults do. They walk out, or they let you down.

He's been standing there so long, he's lost track of the time. He's suddenly aware that there are no more students streaming in. He has to dash, and he just makes it into the room as the bell rings.

Miss Anthony doesn't scold him. She's looking frazzled this morning, and she claps her hands sharply to get their attention.

"Some of you may already know that Mr. Logan has resigned from his teaching job. He wanted me to tell you that he's sorry he didn't have an opportunity to say good-bye to you all, that he'll miss you and he wishes you well. Now, pass your homework forward."

Kevin raises his hand, and the teacher nods in his direction.

"Why did Mr. Logan resign?"

"That's his business, Kevin, not ours."

In his mind, Kevin writes in his journal. *It is my business. He owes me a reason. I believed in him.*

He feels a sharp jab in his shoulder. "Come on, jerk," Eric hisses behind him. "Take the homework."

Kevin grabs the sheets Eric's thrusting at him, adds his own, and passes them forward. Eric's voice is still in his ear.

"Gonna miss Mr. Logan?" he taunts.

Kevin rises and walks up the aisle. "Can I be excused?"

Miss Anthony nods, and he walks out. He starts down the hall toward the restroom, but he stops in front of the principal's office. Maybe he should just pretend to be sick and get out of here.

The secretary's not at her desk. A file is lying there, and it's open to an official looking paper. Kevin's eyes rest on the first line: Logan, Jeffrey. Under that is an address: 628 Maplewood Drive. He remembers the last time he saw that name and address, on a computer screen.

"Can I help you, young man?" The secretary moves alongside him and takes her place behind the desk.

"No, thank you," Kevin says. He catches a brief glimpse of her puzzled face as he whirls around and walks out. He doesn't turn to the right, toward the restroom, or the left, back to his classroom. He walks straight ahead and out the main door.

He walks for half a block before he realizes that he's left his jacket in the class cloakroom. He's lucky he happens to be wearing a heavy sweater. There's a cold wind, but he's too angry to care.

For some reason, an old memory comes to the front

of his mind. He's six, maybe seven years old, and complaining to his mother about something he's not being allowed to do, or have, or whatever. He can see himself now, wailing "It's not fair! It's not fair!" His mother doesn't lose her temper. She doesn't scold him or send him to his room. Her eyes are big and brown and sad as she hugs him close and says, "Life isn't fair, Kevin."

He doesn't think those words meant anything to him at the time. He wishes he'd listened. Maybe if he'd believed her, he wouldn't expect so much from people. Maybe he wouldn't have so many disappointments.

It's a long walk to Maplewood Drive. By the time he gets there, he's still got his anger but he's definitely cold. He checks the numbers on the mailboxes.

There it is, 628. A small white cottage, nothing special. Now that he's here, he begins to have doubts. What's he doing, anyway? What's the point of this? But it's too chilly to stand outside and debate the matter.

Should he knock or ring the bell? As he's trying to decide, the door opens. Unprepared, he stammers. "I—um . . ."

"Hello, Kevin," Mr. Logan says. "I saw you through my window. Come on in. You must be cold." He doesn't act surprised to see him, and he doesn't ask why Kevin's not in school. "Have a seat. Would you like something? Milk? Hot chocolate?"

"No. Thank you," Kevin says stiffly, and he remains standing. He tries not to look at the open suitcase in the living room, the piles of clothes on the sofa, the stack of boxes.

"I'm glad you dropped by." Mr. Logan waves a hand around the mess that surrounds him. "Packing is a pretty boring activity. It's good to have company."

Now Kevin can't pretend to ignore the suitcases and boxes. "You're moving."

"Yes." He moves to face the bookcases, his back to Kevin. "Want to give me a hand with these books?"

Kevin can't believe this. How dare he ask for Kevin's help after what he's done?

When he doesn't respond to Mr. Logan's request, the teacher turns around and faces him.

"You quit," Kevin blurts out.

Mr. Logan nods. "I guess that came as a surprise to you."

That was the understatement of the century, Kevin thinks. Fury rises inside him. "Yeah, no kidding. I thought you had guts. Boy, was I wrong."

He's never spoken so rudely to an adult before. But as far as he's concerned, Mr. Logan doesn't deserve his respect anymore. And his silence only fuels Kevin's anger.

"I'm not the only one who thinks that either! Why did you do it? Why did you let me down?" He'd meant to say *us*. The *me* slipped out. But since it has, he figures he might as well let Mr. Logan know how he feels personally. "I believed in you; I stood up for you!"

"And I appreciate that, but—"

"I thought you were special," Kevin rages. "You're nothing but a coward!" He stops abruptly when he realizes what he's just done. Not only has he interrupted a teacher, he's called him a name! He swallows and shifts his gaze away from Mr. Logan. Has he gone too far?

Mr. Logan doesn't rebuke him. And when he finally speaks, his voice isn't angry or defensive, only sad. "I'm sorry, Kevin. I wish I could have had a chance to tell you myself, and the other kids, too. It wasn't an easy decision to make. Maybe I was afraid you'd try to talk me out of it." A slight smile crosses his face. "I guess that *was* pretty cowardly."

That took the edge off Kevin's fury. He'd never before heard a teacher, or any adult, admit to being afraid. He eyes Mr. Logan warily. "But why did you have to quit? The school board said they wouldn't fire you."

"Well, Kevin, it had to do with more than what the school board would or wouldn't do. I was in a no-win situation and I thought it would be better for everyone if I left."

"I thought you liked teaching us. You *acted* like you did. We thought you were the best P.E. teacher we ever had! Maybe if you had stayed the whole thing would have blown over."

Mr. Logan pushes some clothes aside on the sofa and sits down. "I did like teaching you all. Teaching is what I've always wanted to do, and it means more to me than anything. But I don't think it would have blown over, Kevin. I had to think about the fact that, as a teacher, my first responsibility was to you and the other students. I want you kids to learn. That's why I had to leave."

With Mr. Logan's slow, measured words and the pain that's clearly evident in his eyes, Kevin feels his own anger drain away. What's left is confusion. "I don't get it."

"Kevin, I couldn't teach in that environment. Half the students had been pulled out of P.E. The demonstrators were disrupting your regular class. You weren't getting the instruction you're entitled to."

Kevin can't argue with this. "But you shouldn't have to leave if you wanted to stay. You wanted to stay, didn't you?"

"Yes, I wanted to stay, Kevin. And I *could* have stayed. Many of my friends thought I should."

He rubs his forehead as if he's trying to erase the creases that mark it. "They thought I could become a symbol, to show a community that a person with HIV can continue to work effectively, that we don't put others at risk. Your friend Andy's brother, Jason, said I had an obligation to others with HIV to take a stand. But I had another obligation. To my students. If I stayed and the disruptions continued, it would be at your expense. That wouldn't be fair to you kids."

"Life isn't fair," Kevin mumbles.

"That's right. If life were fair, there wouldn't be wars, or poverty . . . or diseases."

Kevin's having a hard time looking into Mr. Logan's eyes. He focuses on the stack of new boxes.

"So you see, Kevin, I wasn't giving up, I was making a choice. It was a hard choice, but most important choices are. If I stayed, you kids would suffer. So I chose to leave."

Kevin bows his head. As he begins to understand, another emotion takes over. Shame.

"It's my father's fault. Partly, at least." He forces himself to face Mr. Logan. "You must be pretty angry at me."

"I'm not angry at you, Kevin. Why would I hold you responsible for your father's action?"

"He's my father . . ."

Mr. Logan looks thoughtful. "I remember something you said, when we were talking at school once.

When I said your mother left your father, not you, you said it's the same thing. It's not the same thing, Kevin. You're not your father. Did you agree with him? Did you want the school board to fire me?"

"No," Kevin says miserably. "I think he was wrong." He feels tears forming in his eyes. He brushes them away. "I always thought he was perfect, my father."

"You can't expect perfection from anyone, Kevin, not parents, not teachers. Adults are only human beings. They have flaws. If you love them, you accept them, flaws and all. But don't think you can change them, Kevin."

"I wish . . ." Kevin's voice trails off. He's not sure what he was about to wish for.

"If wishes were horses, then beggars would ride," Mr. Logan says.

"My mother used to say that."

Mr. Logan studies him seriously. "You know, Kevin, there are some things in your life that you *can* change. If you're brave enough to try. If you've got the guts. Maybe you can't change the way other people act, but you have control over your own actions."

Kevin wishes he had his journal with him right now. He could write all this down and study it and try to understand. He gets up and wanders over to look at a framed embroidery on the wall. "What's this?"

"A little prayer a friend gave me." Mr. Logan reads

aloud: "Grant me the serenity to accept the things I cannot change, the courage to change the things I can, and the wisdom to know the difference."

"Serenity?"

"Calmness."

"Oh." Kevin looks at the suitcase. "Where are you going?"

"Atlanta."

"My mother lives in Atlanta."

Mr. Logan rises. "Look me up if you're there." He puts out his right hand. Kevin shakes it. "Would you like a ride home?"

"No, thank you. I feel like walking."

"Then take this." Mr. Logan picks up a baseball jacket that was lying on the back of the sofa. "It shrank in the dryer, and it's too small for me. You can keep it, if you like."

"Thanks." Kevin puts it on. It's too big, but he pushes up the sleeves. He pauses at the door.

"You could have stuck it out. Everything might have blown over."

Mr. Logan smiles slightly. "I'm not perfect, either, Kevin. But I had to make a decision. I can only hope I made the right one."

Outside, he walks for a long time. There are a lot of ideas running around in his head. It's going to take him a while to work them out.

He finds himself in front of the police station. Maybe that was where he meant to go. He goes inside, and through the swinging doors.

Charley's not at his desk. Kevin sees that the photo he gave his father for Christmas is there, and he picks it up. He examines the two of them, side by side. Everyone always says he looks just like his father, and he thinks he can see the resemblance. But inside, deep inside, where it counts, do they still resemble each other? He's not so sure anymore.

"Kevin." His father's standing there by his side. "The school just called. Why did you leave?"

"I wasn't feeling good. I mean, I'm not sick, but . . . Mr. Logan quit."

"Yeah, I know."

Kevin bites his lip. "So I guess you won."

Charley shrugs. "Where did you get that jacket?"

"Mr. Logan gave it to me." He steels himself for his father's reaction.

But Charley only nods. Then he reaches out and brushes a lock of hair off Kevin's forehead. "You sure you feel all right?"

Kevin nods.

"Go on home, then. I'll come straight there when I get off at three. I'll pick up a pizza on the way. How does that sound?"

"OK." He starts to leave.

"Kevin?"

He turns back. His father says, "You're a good kid." He looks like he's trying to say a whole lot more.

Back home, Kevin goes straight to his room. He takes off the baseball jacket and hangs it up in his closet, right next to his favorite sweatshirt.

Then he sits down at his desk and opens his journal. Carefully, he tries to record every event of the day. Then he reads it over. He's still not sure what it all means.

He continues writing. "I wonder what's going to happen now. I guess we'll all make up at school and be friends again, but maybe not. I'll try to talk to Eric, but if he acts like a jerk, there's nothing I can do about it. Maybe Mr. Logan won't get AIDS. There's nothing I can do about that, either. My dad—he was all upset about Mr. Logan, but now that he's gone, he acts like he doesn't care. I don't understand. Is there anything I can count on, for sure?"

He thinks for a while. Then he writes "My father loves me."

He sits back and studies the sentence. His father loves him, and he doesn't have to do anything about it, he doesn't even have to agree with everything he says, he just has to love him back. That's not *so* hard. The serenity to accept what you can't change, that's what Mr. Logan said. The courage to change the things you can. The wisdom to know the difference.

He writes: "My mother loves me too." And from memory, he jots down a phone number. He looks at it for a moment. Courage . . . he doesn't have that much. Not yet. He's not ready for talking.

But he doesn't have to call her. There are other ways to begin changing things.

He turns to a fresh, clean page. He grips his pen tightly. And with firm strokes, he writes: "Dear Mom . . ."

FURTHER INFORMATION ABOUT AIDS & HIV

*Having the facts about AIDS and HIV is important for
all of us. If you'd like to know more here are
some places to look.*

BOOKS

Risky Times: How to Be AIDS-Smart & Stay Healthy.
    Jeanne Blake. Workman, 1990.
*One Hundred Questions and Answers about AIDS: A
    Guide for Young People.* Michael Thomas Ford.
    New Discovery Books/Macmillan, 1992.
AIDS: Trading Fears for Facts. Karen Hein. Consumer
    Reports, 1989.

Fifty Things You Can Do about AIDS. Neal Hitchens. Lowell House, 1992.

What You Can Do to Avoid AIDS. Magic Johnson. Times Books, 1992.

My Own Story. Ryan White and Ann Marie Cunningham. Signet, 1992.

NATIONAL HOTLINES

National AIDS Hotline 1-800-342-AIDS

This hotline is run by the Center for Disease Control/ The U.S. Department of Health and Human Services. It's staffed by paid professionals. They can answer questions you have, refer you to all sorts of local organizations, and help you find the most up-to-date printed information about AIDS and HIV. You can call 24 hours a day, 7 days a week.

AIDS Hotline for Teens 1-800-234-TEEN

This hotline is run by an organization called Teens TAP (Teens Teaching AIDS Prevention). It is staffed by high school students who have been trained to answer questions about AIDS and HIV. You can call Monday through Friday from 4 P.M.–8 P.M. Central Standard Time.

National AIDS Clearinghouse 1-800-458-5231

The National AIDS Clearinghouse is run by the Center for Disease Control/The U.S. Department of Health and Human Services. It is equipped with special computer databases that can be searched for the most up-to-date and complete information about resources and services, educational materials, and funding sources for HIV- and AIDS-related service organizations. You can call Monday through Friday from 9 A.M. – 7 P.M. Eastern Standard Time.

OTHER SOURCES

State Hotlines

In addition to the national hotlines there are local hotlines in most states. To get the number of the AIDS hotline in your state call 1-800-555-1212, tell the operator what state you are calling from, and ask the operator to give you the number for the AIDS hotline in that state.

Local Organizations

One way to find out about local organizations is through referrals from a national or state hotline. Your local library or Red Cross chapter may also be able to direct you to local organizations concerned with HIV and AIDS.

Pamphlets

Since new research is being done all the time, pamphlets are an excellent way to get up-to-date information about HIV and AIDS. You may be able to find pamphlets at your local library, or you can request pamphlets from the National AIDS Hotline or the National AIDS Clearinghouse. Many local organizations also publish their own pamphlets, some of which are specifically for young people.

Videos

A number of films and videos have been produced about HIV and AIDS. One of the most famous is *Time Out: The Truth about HIV and AIDS*. It was produced by Paramount Pictures in 1992 and is hosted by Magic Johnson and Arsenio Hall. You can borrow *Time Out* from many video rental stores for free. HBO has also produced a video about AIDS. It's called *AIDS: Everything You and Your Family Need to Know . . . but Were Afraid to Ask* and is hosted by Former U.S. Surgeon General, Dr. C. Everett Koop. You may be able to find *AIDS: Everything You and Your Family Need to Know* at video stores or at your local library.